raise
him up

raise him up

A Single Mother's Guide to Raising a Successful Black Man

BY DERRICK MOORE & STEPHANIE PERRY MOORE

Taken from the Book of Acts

THOMAS NELSON
Since 1798

NASHVILLE DALLAS MEXICO CITY RIO DE JANEIRO

Published in Nashville, Tennessee, by Thomas Nelson. Thomas Nelson is a registered trademark of Thomas Nelson, Inc.

Page design: Crosslin Creative
Images: vectorstock.com, dreamstime.com, istock.com

Thomas Nelson, Inc., titles may be purchased in bulk for educational, business, fund-raising, or sales promotional use. For information, please e-mail SpecialMarkets@ThomasNelson.com.

Unless otherwise noted, Scripture quotations are taken from the KING JAMES VERSION.

ISBN: 9-781-4016-7782-4

Printed in the United States of America

12 13 14 15 QG 6 5 4 3 2 1

Dedication

To
Victor Moore
(Derrick's Brother)

What a blessing a single mother hung
in there and raised you up!

No better brother is there in the world.
Proud of all you've become.

We hope every reader stays her course so
that she too can raise such an awesome man.

Life wasn't always easy for you, but
you listened to your mama

and you turned out alright . . . we love you!

Letter

Hello, our sister,

The Sisters in Faith brand was created to encourage and empower you. As African American women we share a special bond. Our ancestors sacrificed so much for us. As a people we've come so far, yet we know we want to go farther. When we look toward the next generation, our hope in our youth is strong. We want the best for our children. We especially want our males to achieve greatness.

We thought it fitting to have a title for mothers raising sons alone. Sister, if you've picked up this book, you're probably in need of a helping hand to assist you in making sure your son soars. This book was mostly written by a godly, African American man, Derrick Moore. Derrick was raised by a single mother, yet she helped him achieve much with little. That passion with which she raised him is poured into the pages of this book. We pray this guide will inspire you to push your son even harder and strengthen you with biblical nuggets to get your job done.

Above all, we want you to know we care for you, sister. We are thankful you are a mother on the move for God. We are proud you're carrying on. We want this book to help you raise your son.

May the Lord bless you.

—Michele Clark Jenkins & Stephanie Perry Moore
   Sisters in Faith General Editors

Acknowledgements

When you are a single mother raising a son, your task to raise him isn't an easy one. You aren't a male. You have to do it alone. You have to be mother and father. You have to be strong.

Well, when you know God, He lightens your load. He is there to help you. He is there to make sure you are there for your son. The Lord helped us write this book for you. May it bless your soul.

As authors we need help, too. We are raising our hands in thanks to everyone who helps us.

To our parents: Dr. Franklin and Shirley Perry, Sr., and Ann Redding, thanks for raising us up.

To our Publisher and everyone in the Bible, Reference, and Curriculum department: particularly, Bob Sanford, Gary Davidson, Heather McMurray and Alee Anderson, thanks for raising our writing by allowing us this opportunity.

To our extended family: brother, Dennis Perry; sister, Sherry Moore; Godparents, Walter and Marjorie Kimbrough; nephews, Franklin Perry III, and Kadarius Moore; and godsons, Danton Lynn, Dakari Jones, and Dorian Lee, thanks for raising our spirits by always being there.

To our copy editors: Brenda Noel and Dawn Sherill-Porter, of Echo Creative Media, thanks for raising our work to another level with your tireless efforts.

To our friends whom mean so much: Calvin Johnson and the Johnson family, Antonio and Gloria London, Jim and Deen Sanders, Bobby and Sarah Lundy, Kenny Perry, Yolanda Rodgers-Howsie, Pastor Eric and Meik Lee, Pastor James and Jamell Meeks, Pastor Tim Dowdy, Teri Anton, Paul and Susan Johnson, Chan and Laurie Gailey, and Connie Raiford, thanks for raising our hearts with your endearing friendship.

To our teens: Dustyn, Sydni, and Sheldyn, thanks for raising our love to another level as we want God's best for you.

To Stephanie's partner, Michele Clark Jenkins, thanks for raising our creativity to a new level, as this was your idea.

To our new readers, we offer thanks for raising our purpose as we hope this book touches your soul.

And to God, who has given us each other and our dreams, thanks for raising your Son from the dead. Through our faith in Him, we all can be successful.

Table of Contents

Raise Him Up: General Overview

You want your son to make it? You want your son to be all he can be? You want your son to be a successful black man? I know you do. Well, sister, you are the key to making that happen. It may get tough. He may wear you out at times. Your days may be long. But don't give up. Don't send him away. And do not give in. God is with you; and on this side of heaven, no one loves your son as you do. So isn't it worth the investment? You can raise him to be successful, to realize all the dreams that are within him, and to be excellent.

I understand there can be challenges: lack of income, the absence of a male role model in the home, and the peer pressures that come with growing up. These are all realities you may face. With the explosion and popularity of non-scripted programming featuring the real lives of everyday people as they unfold before your very eyes, it can become enticing to trade your own reality for televised reality. Shows like: *The Real Housewives of Atlanta*, *Leave it to Niecey*, and *Basketball Wives* can intrigue you and pull you in; but you have your own reality—a challenging and vital reality. You have the daunting task of raising a son on your own.

The experience of being a single, African American mother is a reality—a non-scripted, real-life experience that only a single, black mother can understand. This book is in your hands to help you. With a biblical twist and a spice of my own experiences, I would like to take you on a journey that will help you provide the passion and purpose for your son to achieve greatness.

Together we will delve into the book of Acts and take notes from the lives of Peter and Paul. This extraction of biblical truth, together with uplifting stories from an exceptional single mother and athletes who encourage us, mixed with an opening motivational part and three inspirational closing points, will reveal the reality that you can raise your son to be significant, successful, and satisfied. The arrangement of this book was created to warm your heart and encourage your soul, for I feel where you are.

I know you can do it! I was raised by a hard–working, single mother who gave everything to make sure my brother, sister, and I would have a chance at success. The choices we sometimes made didn't make things easy for my mom. Life didn't make things easy for her because our circumstances were difficult. And God didn't make it easy because He wanted her to take up her cross daily and follow Him. She was steadfast; you can be, too. Keeping your eyes on the reward of seeing your son be all he can be will give you the strength and determination you need. You *can* raise him, my sister!!!

show him the power of Peter

Every young brother can take notes from the Apostle Peter. Something set this man on fire! Was it something internal; was it something external, or was it both? Was it something he saw or something he heard? Was it something he did or simply something he felt? Whatever it was, I know it had him fired up! Peter realized the power inside of him to do great things, even things that seemed impossible. When the impossible becomes possible, there is no challenge too great.

Actually, you have the type of power Peter had. I clearly see you, working through the day to help your son make it. You have an overwhelming belief that he can achieve greatness and you won't rest until you feel he has arrived. Oh, no. No time for afternoon naps. No alarm clocks are needed. No one has to remind you. You are on a mom mission like no other; you won't give in; you won't give out; and you won't give up. Simply put, you're just plain ole fired up to raise him right.

Mothers have power to influence the direction their children are headed. Your son needs you to teach him to exude power. Whether he is three or thirty, the quicker he gets fired up (like you are for him and like Peter was for Jesus), the sooner he will find his way and make you both proud.

I commend you for your heart. Helping your child is worth everything to you. So you are leaving nothing on the table; and there is no turning back. This book is a one-way-ticket designed to help you get your child to the destination you desire for him; it is a guidebook to help you enable your son to apprehend all that God has for him.

If I wanted to find a single Bible character who epitomizes the concept of being fired up, I would have to look no further than Jesus Himself. With the passion of a devoted father, Jesus leapt into the chaotic. Not because He had to, but because He wanted to. Jesus willingly left His Father's side in order to get next to ours. Jesus was fired up because we needed Him; our sinful, needy condition required all His concentration, all His determination, and more importantly, all His love. From the time John the Baptist proclaimed "I indeed baptize you with water unto repentance. But he that cometh after me is mightier than I, whose shoes I am not worthy to bear: he shall baptize you with the Holy Ghost, and with fire" as Jesus was baptized, to the time when Jesus cried out from the cross, "Eli, Eli, lama sabachthani?" (which means, "My God, my God, why hast thou forsaken me?"), Jesus had unparalleled power to help. At these times, as well as all times in between, Jesus displayed the power to help us like no other. So should your power to help you son be a power like no other.

Having been raised by a single mom, I know life as the sole provider for your son can get tough sometimes. Hold on; Jesus is there. That's right; I said it. You are the one who keeps the Lord up all night, longing to be in sweet fellowship with Him. To be completely honest, He is as fired up about you today as He was the moment He laid eyes on you. He knows your struggles, woes, and problems. He cares and He will see you through; much like the endless effort you pour out for your son.

Now, if Jesus isn't an example to whom you can relate, let's consider one who may be closer to you by way of humanity. Let's consider the life of Peter—one of the most influential writers of the New Testament. Why was he so fired up? Something happened to him as he encountered Jesus and others that caused him to live a life of incredible power for what he believed.

Peter's excitement is contagious. Come and be amazed at his powerful life. His life exemplifies what it means to be fired up for something you love and to be able to walk in that power on a daily basis.

The dreams that are within your son can be reached. Greatness can be his. The Lord has a calling on both your lives that He wants you both to obtain.

In Part I of this guide, we will delve into the power of Peter as he believed in the right thing. These first six chapters will help you guide your son to stay the course. Read along; and let's keep you excited to see him grow in power to reach his goals!

wasting no time

Teach him

to not

procrastinate.

(Taken from Acts 2:14–21)

 Motivational Point

Before we can teach others a subject, we must first master it ourselves. However, I'm talking to a super mom. You are on the ball. How to be a mom is a subject you know well, right?

Let's begin with a little riddle. What hangs on a wall, has twelve numbers, a short hand, a long hand, and makes a tick-tock sound? I can see there's no tricking you, my sister. Of course, it's a clock.

Oh, Father Time—that ever-present, ever-passing, ever-dominating element of life. We can try to manage it; for certain, we can't control it. Time continues at a steady pace that never changes. It doesn't discriminate. It doesn't respect any person, and we're all given the same amount on any given day. Sixty seconds in every minute. Sixty minutes in every hour. The hours turn into days; the days turn into weeks; the weeks turn into months; and before you know it, months have turned into years. And oh, how fast the years roll by! I'm sure your baby boy isn't a baby anymore. Where do the years go?

Therefore, not wasting time is the first lesson we need to make sure your son masters. Whatever he does in life, he is up against the clock, so he must get to it—homework, SAT testing, getting into college, finding a job, and the list goes on. As his mother, you must take seriously your duty to call him on to greater things. Your urging must be done now. If he's in preschool, it's time to urge him on. If he's in elementary school, encourage him to excel. If he's in middle school, exhort him to press harder. When high school days arrive, challenge him to give it all he's got. Even when your son passes that magic age of eighteen, do not stop urging him to surpass expectations.

Don't allow your son to put off the journey to success. Exhort him to get on the path to success today. Putting it off will only give him less of an opportunity to attain the dream and waiting will only push the dream further away. Time is of the essence and every precious second counts. Procrastination is the enemy of opportunity. Opportunity is what you have in your possession. Your son is your opportunity to dream of what *can* be in spite of what has been.

What has been your story? Very few resources? Limited access? Sleepless nights? Begin focusing on what *can* be: many resources, limitless access, and nights of peaceful rest. You can't delay because you've been denied. Instead, you have to demand of your son and of yourself that the dream will live and not die. Never mind what is missing. It only matters what is present. So get to it, mom. Begin moving him in the direction of his destiny, and don't let circumstances or people around you talk you out of it. Be dedicated and determined to arrive at the place where your dreams live. I know, with this mind set, your efforts will be rewarded and your dreams for your son will be realized. (This is not a solo effort. You may be a single mother, but you are not raising him on your own. The God of the Bible is an expert on parenting. I think He knows a little about raising a son.)

So, dear sister, you are facing what is called the "tyranny of the urgent." You see, the urgent demands you give whatever you have to meet a challenge . . . right now! You can't wait to make your move. So now that you have your goal for your son in your sight, you have to seize the moment. While it is true time marches relentlessly on, this moment can mark the beginning of a profound life change. If you can help your son capture the moment, he can capture his dreams. The opportunity is here and you are ready! This moment can make time stand still as your son's dream comes into view. Now that's time management! Nothing wasted, everything gained, and no procrastination!

 ## Spiritual Impact

THE STORY OF PETER'S FIRST SERMON

(Acts 2:14–21)

Right after Jesus sent the Holy Spirit to empower His church, Peter became a force to be reckoned with.

> But Peter, standing up with the eleven, lifted up his voice, and said unto them, Ye men of Judaea, and all ye that dwell at Jerusalem, be this known unto you, and hearken to my words. (Acts 2:14)

TIME OUT!

You may wonder why I'm calling a "time out." Well, in sports, a time out signifies a moment of great importance.

Peter gave us a powerful truth, right off the bat: if you're going to help your son capture the dream of success, you first better find the courage to stand up, raise your voice, and proclaim the victory. Got it?

With most sermons, the audience is equipped with a title for the message. A title is normally given for the sole purpose of providing a sense of direction. The intention of the speaker is to relate everything—the introduction, the body, and the—conclusion—back to the title. All a speaker says illuminates the title of his message.

TIME OUT!

More than anything, your son needs your guidance. Look at it this way, if success is the title of your dreams for your son, all the guidance you give him should illuminate and clarify the title for him. Make sense?

Peter, being the passionate apostle to the Jews, wasted no time in referring to an Old Testament prophecy (Joel 2:28–31). Peter quoted a passage that was quite significant to the Jewish people about God pouring out His Spirit on them.

> For these are not drunken, as ye suppose, seeing it is but the third hour of the day. But this is that which was spoken by the prophet Joel; And it shall come to pass in the last days, saith God, I will pour out of my Spirit upon all flesh: and your sons and your daughters shall prophesy, and your young men shall see visions, and

your old men shall dream dreams: And on my servants and on my handmaidens I will pour out in those days of my Spirit; and they shall prophesy: And I will shew wonders in heaven above, and signs in the earth beneath; blood, and fire, and vapour of smoke: The sun shall be turned into darkness, and the moon into blood, before that great and notable day of the Lord come: And it shall come to pass, that whosoever shall call on the name of the Lord shall be saved. (Acts 2:15–21)

Peter was so fired up that he reached into Old Testament prophesy to tell everyone that salvation is available to any who call on the name of the Lord. Peter was determined to get his message across. To do so, he used everything at his disposal to reach those who listened. He poured out his heart and exhausted every means to bring life to all who would come.

TIME OUT!

The question is: how willing or determined are you to exercise your power for your dream of raising your son? Will you pour your heart and soul into your fight on his behalf? Will you put into use all the tools at your disposal to reach your son and call him forth into the destiny God has prepared for him?

In the case of Peter's first sermon, the title is not mentioned; however, it can be concluded from his introduction. If a title were assigned to Peter's sermon, it could be called, *An Inside Job*! Peter's message expounds on the inner working of the Holy Spirit and the outward impact He will have on a surrendered life.

After the introduction was given, Peter got right to the body of his message. With his straight-to-the-point, no-beating-around-the-bush approach, he unapologetically expressed to the people of Israel present that day that it was God's plan for Jesus to die for the sin of the world and to then be raised from the dead. This meant that those who crucified Jesus did so within the foreknowledge and plan of God. But the evil intent of man resulted in the coming of the promised Holy Spirit—the One who would live and dwell in the hearts of all believers.

Peter's conclusion was quite simple—Jesus, the man crucified, was the Messiah.

> Therefore let all the house of Israel know assuredly, that God hath made the same Jesus, whom ye have crucified, both Lord and Christ. Now when they heard this, they were pricked in their heart, and said unto Peter and to the rest of the apostles, Men and brethren, what shall we do? (Acts 2:36, 37)

Peter then went on to present to his listeners the way of applying the truth he had spoken to them—repent and be baptized.

> Then Peter said unto them, Repent, and be baptized every one of you in the name of Jesus Christ for the remission of sins, and ye shall receive the gift of the Holy Ghost. For the promise is unto you, and to your children, and to all that are afar off, even as many as the LORD our God shall call. (Acts 2:38, 39)

Peter extended the same invitation we have all received: to come and be saved from the power of sin and death and be granted access to the throne of Almighty God by way of Jesus' death on the cross.

TIME OUT!

Seize this nugget of urgency for your son's future. Start working toward those goals right now. Go! Do it! Start! Sister, what are you waiting for? Peter got right to it. You do the same; and don't let your son waste a moment!

Mama's Story:

THE STORY OF WHEN WAITING WOULDN'T WORK

Lesson: Don't wait; do all that can be done.

I will never forget the day my mother taught me the importance of not wasting time. I was in my freshman year of college and had walked away from a scholarship because I just felt something else was out there for me. You see, I wanted to play professional football. But, because I had not peeked athletically in high school, the big Division 1 schools passed me by.

Even though it was no big-name school, my mother was elated when Albany State University, a college in our home town, gave me a shot on their football team. She could still watch me; she could still feed me; she could still cheer me on—all because I was close to home. Nonetheless, because I wanted to play and a great number of players with more seniority were standing in my way, I decided to leave. You see, because of my mother's influence I have never been the sitting-around type.

Immediately after that tough choice, I wondered if I had made a big mistake. But, my mother would not let me sulk in my confusion. Absolutely not! She told me the clock was ticking and what was done was done. She told me God was with me either way; and since I'd chosen this new path, I'd better get to moving so He could bring me to my blessing. She told me sitting around on my hands was not going to teach me anything; she said I needed to use them. Taking in her words, I trained harder. I kept believing that one day I'd need to show the new coaches I knew my way around the gridiron.

I went to a junior college immediately after Albany State. I understood that I needed to stay in school so I'd be on track academically when I got my next opportunity. And I stayed in God's word, realizing that, with Him, I could do all things.

It was only a year and a half later when I got the call to walk on (to come to school without a scholarship) at Troy State. We were poor and the cost at Troy was high; but God—provided—a bank granted me a student loan that would cover all my expenses.

You know, when you get to the business at hand, God shows His hand and works miracles. When I got to Troy and worked out for the coaches, they were so impressed with my character, my past semester grades, and mostly, my skills, they gave me a full scholarship. My mom wasted no time before proudly returning the student loan check to the bank.

She told me I could do it. She told me not to waste a second doubting. She told me God would see me through. She was right. Thank God I listened.

Sister, teach your son to not procrastinate. Keep pushing him until he moves on his own. The results awaiting him are overwhelming. Press on!

Athletic Tale (to share with your son)

FRANK REICH, THE COMEBACK KID

Sports stories motivate and inspire us to achieve. In this portion, I am excited to share an athletic account that moved me and helped me learn to never waste precious time. Now girl, I know you might not be the athletic type and this jargon may not connect with you, but hang in there. I believe this story (and the ones like it in the next eleven chapters) will still touch you, sister, and give you something encouraging to share with your son.

It is said lightening doesn't strike twice in the same place; and I agree with that saying. However, in the case of now-retired, football player, Frank Reich, it did exactly as it reportedly will not do; it struck resoundingly in the same place twice—two different cities, two different teams, two different stadiums. The center of the duplicate activity was Frank, a quarterback who made history. I can call a time out here if you need me too. Okay, let's keep going.

Nearly a decade apart, two of the most improbable comebacks would take place. What made them improbable

weren't the games themselves, but the man who orches-
trated them both while snatching victory from the hands of
defeat. The words of offensive guru, Ralph Friedgen, spoken
about Frank Reich to Reich's father were nearly prophetic,
"Frank's going to have to be ready. He'll have to come in
and win a game for us."

Frank Reich attended the University of Maryland on a
football scholarship. Early in the 1984 season, Reich suffered
a separated shoulder and lost his starting quarterback position. Stan Gelbaugh replaced him. Gelbaugh was playing well,
so there was no need to reinsert Frank, even though he had
healed from his injury. Frank learned firsthand how coaches
favor whichever quarterback is flourishing at the moment; and
early in 1984, that favored quarterback wasn't Frank Reich.

However, on November 10, 1984, at the old Orange Bowl
Stadium, Frank was brought off the bench to play for Stan Gelbaugh. Frank's team was down 31 to 0, and there were only
thirty minutes left in the game against Miami. Whatever Frank
had to do, he needed to get it done quickly. He realized he
had two enemies: one, the Miami Hurricanes, and the other,
ole Father Time. Time was short and the seconds ticked mercilessly away, but a lightning strike was about to happen.

During the third quarter, Frank led the Maryland Terra-
pins on multiple scoring drives. Three touchdowns in the third
quarter and a fourth at the start of the final quarter turned
what was a blowout into a close game. With the score at

34 to 28, with Miami leading, Frank led his team to one final, amazing touchdown and Maryland won the game 42 to 40. Reich had led his team to the most incredible comeback in NCAA history.

Lightening would also strike a second time while he was playing for the Buffalo Bills. Frank would lead the Bills back from what appeared to be an insurmountable lead by the then Houston Oilers. Both teams had made the playoffs as wild card teams. What was ironic was that the two teams had met in the final, pre-season game with Buffalo being defeated by Houston 27 to 3 in Houston. They weren't supposed to have a chance.

Houston completely dominated the first quarter with quarterback, Warren Moon, taking a 28 to 3 halftime lead. Compounding the problem, the Bills and Reich would start the second half by throwing an interception that was returned for a touchdown by the other team.

Talk about going from bad to worse! The Bills were in trouble of enormous status. Down 35 to 3 and less than fourteen minutes left in the third quarter, Frank and the Buffalo Bills began to mount a comeback. If you know anything about Buffalo football at Rich Stadium, it is famous for gusting winds that blow tremendously. It seemed upon the ensuing kick-off, that not fate, but faith would have it so that the squib kick would travel no further than the fifty yard line.

TIME OUT!

The definition of a squib kick is a football kickoff in which the ball bounces along the ground.

Ten plays later, Frank threw a touchdown and continued to lead the team to tie the score and send the game into overtime.

Houston won the coin toss and would get the ball first, but to no avail. The ball was intercepted. The Bills and Frank Reich moved the ball for a few more yards to set up the game winning field goal. Frank Reich finished the game with a 21 of 34 passing day, 289 yards, and 4 touchdowns to lead the Bills to a virtually impossible comeback. Well, unless you were Frank Reich and the Buffalo Bills. Now that's getting right to it!

Sports stories may not be your thing; but sports are a way of reaching and teaching young men. Frank Reich's story shows so clearly how important it is to stay the course, even in the face of seemingly insurmountable odds. Pursuing a dream and pushing toward that winning life goal may not be easy; it may require that your son face down others who consider his dream impossible. Others may even count him out. But if you keep encouraging your son to strive for sweet victory, if you cheer him on in the face of threatened defeats, you can watch with pride as he overcomes all obstacles and captures the win for himself and his life.

Inspirational Insight
Stephanie's Message

Wow, sister! I hope you were inspired by the first four parts of chapter one. I know I was. Derrick has helped me see that time certainly plays a major factor in the outcome of many of life's experiences.

Wise management of time is critical as you pursue your dreams. Therefore, it is crucial to teach your son to have a driving passion for making the most of his time. Setting a course and making every minute count as he pursues his destiny is a powerful formula for success.

Here are three Inspirational Insights to help you lead your son to sweet victory:

First, *teach him to know what he wants and to want it badly.* Help your son hone in on his dream. You can never underestimate the "want to" factor. Once your son has allowed his dream to grab hold of him, his desire will give birth to the passion required to attain it. When your son embraces his dream with a passion to see it come true, it will be much easier for you, as his mom, to help him work toward that dream. Not only must you lead your son to have faith that his dream is attainable, you must teach him to put work behind that faith. Simply put, faith without works is dead. Teach your son that work will demonstrate faith and faith will produce the desired result.

Secondly, *teach him to not worry about the score*. Looking up at the scoreboard can discourage your son from pursuing his dream. No matter where he is on his journey, it will continually seem to him that he is behind. Teach him to simply keep his head in the game. When he learns to pursue his dream with a total disregard for the scoreboard, lookout! If he pursues with all he has, the score will take care of itself. Teach your son to pay little attention to the scoreboard, but to keep his eyes on the prize—the realization of his dream.

Finally, *teach him to focus on one play at a time*. The meaning of this old cliché mirrors the equally old saying, "one step at a time." Life happens one play, or one step, at a time. Help your son understand he can't live in the future; only the present has any bearing on real life. Whatever is happening right now determines the play that must be run. Focusing on the next ten plays will only cause the here and now to suffer. Help your son understand the importance of concentrating on the play (or situation) of the moment. Finding success today will increase the probability of success tomorrow.

Well, time keeps ticking away. Remember, the clock never stops. By the same token, it will never skip a beat. As we close this session, I encourage you to keep on laboring on your son's behalf. Be the mom, the dad, the teacher, the doctor, the preacher, and anything else he needs to help him arrive at his dream. Yes, it will be hard work; I know . . . Derrick says he made it rough for his mom sometimes, too. But thanks to his praying, pushing, powerful mother and a God who shows mercy, he became something.

So don't give up. One day your efforts will be rewarded. Your son will arrive at the amazing, unique destiny God chose specifically for him. Then you can rejoice, knowing you helped him seize every hour, every minute, and every second . . . nothing wasted! **Raise him, sister!!!**

give what you have

Teach him to not sit on his talent.

(Taken from Acts 3:1–6)

 Motivational Point

As a single mom working hard for your son, you are an expert in giving. You live by the motto: his needs first, yours second. If he needs a hug and you're tired, you give it. If he needs help with homework and you are exhausted, you give it. If he needs discipline and your heart wants to be lenient, you "woman up" and give him the correction he needs. You press on through personal shortcomings and negative feelings, and you stretch yourself for the better outcome for your child. Well, that's fabulous, sister. Now, your son needs to have that same mentality. We want him to give his all, too. Let's get him there.

One of the most respected men I have ever known in the world of sports was the Special Teams' coach during my time with the Detroit Lions, the late, great Frank Ganz. He was just an all-around tremendous human being. Sister, you would have loved him. He was a fair man who lived to see his team thrive. He was most famous for his powerful quotes. My favorite was, "What you give will grow. What you keep, you'll lose."

Oops! I almost forgot; I don't want to get ahead of myself.

TIME OUT!

"Special teams" are units typically considered the third wheel on a football team. There is offense, defense, and special teams.

The reason I share with you Coach Ganz' quote is that you have a whole lot to give your son, my sister. What you give him today will grow within him throughout his life. If you teach him to care, share, and dare while he is young, he will reap the results of the right thinking you instill in him as he grows.

The most powerful inspiration you can give your son is to continually show him the sacrificial love you pour out daily to enable him to go after his dreams. This type of giving is called a living sacrifice. It's the kind of giving that may set you back, but the kind that will set him up. It may be that you sacrificed some of the money needed for the months' expenses so your son could participate in a camp to further develop his skills as an individual. You may have sacrificed dollars set aside for your hair and nails, so he could get new school clothes. You may choose to pay for a tutor for your son with the cash you've put aside for months to get a car tune-up. You forego trips to places you long to see in order to provide everything your son needs. Yes, you give and give for him, sister. God bless you.

You make difficult choices, reasoning that you will find a way to replace the money, somehow. In one way, these choices are setbacks; but they are also set ups. You may bear the struggle alone; but you will share the victories and successes with that young man you adore. You give so he can receive. Difficult? Yes! Rewarding? Most definitely! How incredibly fulfilling it can be to know you successfully bear the weight of responsibilities that are typically shared by a mate in the home. Your role is a heavy one, yet you manage alone. And you succeed alone. Go, sister!

You give freely to your son; and that is right and good. But your son needs to give back. He needs to do his part. When he senses that he holds a place of importance in your life, you will gain his attention. When he realizes you expect things from him in return, his favorable response will blow your mind. If you need to get his attention about school, you'll have it. If you need to get his attention about friends, you'll have it. When he knows you put him first (after God, of course), he will began to truly understand your commitment to him, and he will be much more open to your guidance and more receptive to your expectations. Make sure your son understands that you take care of him because you love him. Teach him that love is an active verb—to be real, it must direct his actions. Lead him to make a commitment to a life of love early on. Help him understand that commitment is not a sometimes thing, it's an all-the-time thing. Who knows where the ability to make a commitment could lead him as he travels down the road to his future? Don't be hesitant to use your influence; you earned it by your sacrificial love.

The willingness to give he's seen in you will foster a personal initiative on his behalf to maximize what he has been given by and through you. His appreciation will help him take full responsibility for developing his own talent and potential. He will see the value in his giftings because you see the value in him. If he sees his own value through your eyes, he will be much more likely to put in the work it takes to excel. It's great to have talent, but people with the will to work their talent will out-work talent alone any day of the week.

Don't allow your son to fall into the trap that snares so many talented people; don't let him fall under the spell of entitlement. People who consider themselves entitled by their gifts and abilities don't want to work. They want life handed to them on a silver platter. Teach your son to maximize all he is through a great work ethic. If he's struggling in an area, encourage him to keep working on it. If he's excelling in something, push him to excel all the more. Whatever abilities he has, teach him to work in order to enjoy the increase. To quote Todd Blackledge, a former college and professional quarterback, "Work will win when wishing won't." Teach your son these six Ws to success.

Giving your son all you have is great. But he has to deserve it. If the chores aren't done, if the grades aren't good, if the attitude is off, then it is only right to withhold any reward. Sister, if you give a flower water, but not too much of it, it'll grow. If you give it some sunshine, but not too much of it, it'll grow. And if you give your son enough of you with just the right mix of responsibility on his part, he'll grow so high he'll touch the sky.

 Spiritual Impact

THE STORY OF PETER AND JOHN HEALING A LAME MAN

(Acts 3:1–6)

One day Peter and John were going up to the temple at the time of prayer at three in the afternoon. Now a man who was lame from birth was being carried to the temple gate called Beautiful, where he was put every day to beg from those going into the temple courts. When he saw Peter and John about to enter, he asked them for money. Peter looked straight at him, as did John. Then Peter said, "Look at us!" So the man gave them his attention, expecting to get something from them. Then Peter said, "Silver or gold I do not have, but what I do have I give you. In the name of Jesus Christ of Nazareth, walk" (Acts 3:1–6).

There was something I found to be curious about this text. The lame beggar never asked to be healed. He only asked for money.

And a certain man lame from his mother's womb was carried, whom they laid daily at the gate of the temple which is called Beautiful, to ask alms of them that entered into the temple; Who seeing Peter and John about to go into the temple asked an alms. (Acts 3:2, 3)

What this man wanted and what he needed were two very different things. The real issue was not that he was a beggar needing money; the core issue was that this man was lame. Rather than a few measly, charitable coins, what he needed was the ability to earn his own. Peter and John saw beyond the request to the need. They didn't allow the beggar's words to cloud the issue. And they provided far more than the beggar could even have thought to ask.

Often, your son's requests will be based on his wants; he may not be even faintly aware of his actual needs. Your ability to see your son's greater need is key to his development. It's very important that you stay disciplined. Don't get caught up in attempting to give what your son wants; instead, give him what he needs. If you get sidetracked trying to provide what he wants, you may never give him what he needs. You see, your son's greater need is you! Not the things you can or can't give.

> And Peter, fastening his eyes upon him with John, said, Look on us. And he gave heed unto them, expecting to receive something of them. Then Peter said, Silver and gold have I none; but such as I have give I thee: In the name of Jesus Christ of Nazareth rise up and walk. (Acts 3:4–6)

Peter and John saw beyond the beggar's wants into his true needs. They did not allow the minor issue to overshadow the major one. They were not fooled by the beggar's focus on the more irrelevant issue. In the same way, your son will sometimes attempt to make the irrelevant issue the focus; but your task is to always target the relevant issue. Sister, make sure you always stick to the point. Don't let him get you off track.

By being a channel of healing for the lame beggar, Peter and John became instruments of true enabling. The chain reaction of lameness to poverty was broken because these two godly men saw beyond want into true need. The beggar's reaction was to leap to his feet and praise God for all he was worth. His healing became his liberation and was a witness of God's power to all who stood and watched.

Your ability to show your son his needs over his wants is a powerful thing. Powerful because you are enabling him to walk toward his dreams and not settle for begging you for the lesser things in life. When he is equipped he can work toward the greater things life holds. Target the heart of the matter and then stand back. Watch him get up and go after whatever he wants out of life. Watch him study longer. Watch him train harder. And watch him care deeper.

Mama's Story:

THE STORY OF HOMEMADE FLAPJACKS

Lesson: Just because you don't see it doesn't mean it's not there.

My mom was at work. The three of us—my older brother, my younger sister, and I—were three hungry mice who could not even find a slice of cheese. It wasn't all that unusual for us to have very little to nothing to eat. But, according to my mother, we always had something to tide us over. On this particular day, my mother was gone and we found ourselves hungry at home without any money. (Now, if you can relate to this story at any level just say, "Amen!")

We decided the only thing we could do was to call our mom and hope she could fix the problem. You see, we were hoping she would point us to some money hidden under a mattress or something. But that's not what she did at all.

Now, before I tell you what she did, let me say we were absolutely positive there was nothing in that house to eat—nothing in the refrigerator, nothing in the cabinets, and nothing on the stove. The only things we could find were a half bag of flour, a half bottle of syrup, and a small stick of butter in the refrigerator. To us, that looked like nothing.

When we called mom, she said, "Y'all look up in the cabinets and take down that bag of flour. Pour the flour into a bowl. Now, take a glass of water and pour enough of it into the bowl with the flour and stir it so that it gets a little soupy. Now, take a pan from the bottom cabinet and place it on the stove. Take a little butter and put it in the pan. Turn the stove on medium. Now, pour the mixed flour into the pan and cook it on both sides until it is done inside and out. After you're done, take the syrup and pour it on the flapjacks; that will tide you over until I get home."

My mother was great at giving what she had and not complaining about what she didn't have. If she couldn't buy new clothes, she just kept the ones we had clean. If she had no transportation, she found a way to get where she needed to be—sometimes utilizing ways others would deem beneath them. No matter what the need, she found a way to get it done. I can tell you this: I have never eaten a pancake that had anything on my mother's flapjacks. She called them the kind of food that "sticks to your ribs." If she was committed to anything, she was truly committed to never letting us go hungry. If we had nothing, we were going to eat somehow or some way.

It's easy to look around us and see that others have more and start to get discouraged. But when you come to recognize whatever you have to give is enough, that's when you know you are going to make it. My mom teases with me to this day, saying if she had possessed all I have today, there is no telling what she could have done.

Sister, there is a lot to be said for that. Concentrate on using everything you have to get your son where you want him to be. Spend no time on trying to give what you don't have.

My mother revealed to me a talent that I never knew I had: the ability to make something from nothing. It's a talent I have used in every endeavor of my life. Just take what you have, use it wisely, and watch how far it goes.

When your son can't go to the movies, watch the television with him. When the television is out, have him read a book. When the library is closed, tell him stories and play board games with him. In all those scenarios, one thing is the same: fun is there to be had for your son. If you teach him to wisely use what he has, he'll be alright.

 Athletic Tale

THE WORK ETHIC OF JERRY RICE

I am convinced that we all have different skill sets. Some can run faster than others, and some can cook better than others. Nevertheless, in a world where everyone seems to be looking for an edge, I summit to you there is one sizable advantage that makes the difference—creating success for some and failure for others. You don't have to be born from a particular family; you don't need to have a lot of money; it doesn't matter who you know or don't know. It only matters that you are willing to roll up your sleeves and decide you are going to outwork anybody and everybody who's competing with you.

Jerry Rice was such a person. I had the brief opportunity to spend a training camp with the San Francisco 49ers of the NFL. What I learned in that short time changed my perception of work. You see, I thought work was just completing a task list for the day—making sure everything got done. I learned quickly that it isn't about getting things done; it's about how you get them done and what they look like once completed. No one exemplified this work ethic mentality quite like Jerry Rice. Jerry had enormous athletic ability. But I truly believe it paled in comparison to how he worked at his craft. He wasn't just satisfied with running a route; he had to run a perfect route.

TIME OUT!

Let me make sure you know what Jerry Rice did for a living. He was the greatest wide receiver to ever play the game of football. He caught passes thrown to him by two of the greatest quarterbacks in NFL history, Joe Montana and Steve Young.

Jerry Rice was one of the best wide receivers ever because he did more than he was asked. He studied positions other than his. He ran longer than anyone. He just worked, worked, and then worked some more.

If your son is going to be good at anything, please challenge him to have this kind of work ethic. You can promise him it won't return void. Assure him his hard work will produce amazing results if he maximizes every opportunity to become better.

Sister, some people work and some people work hard. Jerry Rice worked hard, and the proof could be seen by all in his incredibly successful career. The same holds true for your son. If he will work hard at his dream, results will follow. There is always real, tangible proof of hard work. Proof of hard work is not found in the fact that you have reached a certain level of success; instead, the proof exists in the eyes of the people who saw you work hard to excel. I think what still amazes me about Jerry Rice even more than his accomplishments (Super Bowl champion, MVP, and being recognized as the greatest receiver to ever play the game) is the incredible amount of hard work he was willing to exert to achieve those things. Daily, he gave his all.

I am convinced that, if you teach your son the real value of working for what he wants and encourage him to work harder than the competition, one day he will stand in the company of greatness. I know it feels good when you give him the latest toy, new sneakers, or a cool car. But, sister, the thrill of those gifts will come to a very quick end for you and for him. When you teach your son to push himself 100% every day in everything, you've given him a gift that will keep on giving throughout his life.

Inspirational Insight
Stephanie's Message

As I read this chapter, my heart broke knowing Derrick's upbringing was so very different from mine. My cupboards were overflowing. My parents even frequently took my younger brother and me to the finest restaurants. Why did Derrick have it so tough? You may be asking why things are so tough for you. As I kept reading my husband's story, I was overjoyed by the reminder that God shows up in tough times. He did it for Derrick, and He will most certainly do the same for you.

If you give all you have, then guess what? It will always be enough. I found three powerful points in the chapter above. I guarantee you they are a formula for success in raising your son. In the points below, your son's "pocket" stands for all the things he carries with him through life.

First, *teach him that what's in his pocket counts*. You are there to help him fill his pockets with opportunity and accomplishments. Empty pockets lead nowhere. If there is nothing in his pocket, you need to help him fill it with valuable things.

The first thing that belongs in his pocket is a little self-respect. He needs to care about who he is, as his mother's son; and whose he is, as a child of God. The moment he becomes proud of his identity, he will begin to build the cornerstone of a successful and significant life. What other building blocks do you believe your son needs to equip him to build a life of purpose and meaning? Start helping him fill his pockets with the standards and virtues upon which he can depend throughout his life. But don't forget the foundation: a healthy relationship with the Lord.

Secondly, *teach him that he can have confidence in the things in his pocket*. Derrick told you that it took a lot of hard work to accomplish greatness. Every time your son reaches a place of achievement, help him grab hold of the confidence he can have as a result. Not in arrogance; but with the confidence that comes from putting in enough work to excel. Your son has the right to be confident when he has earned what he now owns. His achievements are valuable tools to be kept in his pocket.

Finally, *teach him to always be on the lookout for new and beneficial things to keep in his pocket*. Help him be watchful for the useful and valuable things that can improve and add to his life. The enemy of success is complacency. Don't let your son get distracted because of success; instead, help him learn to use each success as a stepping stone to the next. Help him stay focused and see his life as a continual journey. If he stops along the way, he will never know how much he could have achieved.

We are only two chapters into this book and I am excited to apply the information toward raising my son. Just this morning, he was complaining about his lunch choices. He said there was no food. There was plenty; but he had to work to prepare it and that wasn't appealing to him. However, he decided going hungry was worse than a little effort. So he boiled some eggs, opened a tuna can, cut up an onion, got out the relish and mayo, and then mixed it all together in a bowl. Amazing! Tuna salad made by his own two hands! He got good and full. I could have come to his rescue. But I decided to teach him to do for himself. His own efforts resulted in a satisfying meal, and he was proud of himself.

It's in our DNA as mothers to give until we have no more. But, we must also remember it is our job to teach our sons to help themselves. Use wisdom to know when to step up and when to step back. Give him what he needs, but don't forget to teach him to be self-sufficient. **Raise him, sister!!!**

questioned by others

Teach him to not let others sidetrack his dreams.

(Taken from Acts 4:1–22)

Motivational Point

It seems there are more questions in life than there are answers. Where am I going to get the money to pay the bills? How is my son going to get an opportunity to go to college? When am I going to find a job that pays enough for me to take a vacation? And then there are the kinds of questions that demoralize the spirit. Who do you think you are? How are you going to pay for that stuff? Don't you know that it's your fault? Well, sister, you don't need to worry about the questions. You just need to be courageous enough to address them.

Now, the latter of these questions can cause you to get defensive; but keep your composure, sister. I know what can happen when someone gets on your nerves. Don't let the questions get you out of your comfort zone. At all times, stay the course and respond with class. I do recognize that some questions should not be dignified with a response; but if you do need to respond, just know that you not only have the courage to do so, but you also have the confidence that comes with it.

There are those inside your world, namely family members or close relatives, who are going to question your efforts and even your methods. They may hound you with questions: "Why do you spoil him so?" or "Why are you so hard on him?" or "I know you don't plan to introduce that man to your son, right?" You know family means well; but sometimes it would be nice if they would keep all the nit-picking comments to themselves.

Friends and close acquaintances have their questions, as well: "Why are you paying for golf lessons when you're barely making it?" or "You got some money stashed away; when are you going to pay for a tutor?" or "Why did you buy a new dress when your son's shoes are torn up?" They are just all in your business.

Do not let their questions get you off track. You have a mission to get your son from one place in life to the next. It does not matter what questions others may have. It only matters that you can answer every single one of them. You spoil him because you love him. You get on his case because you don't want him ever locked out of the American dream. You have learned who and who not to let your son meet. You dig and pay for golf lessons, so the game can teach him life lessons. You'll pay for the tutor when your son does his part in class. And you bought yourself a dress because you worked for it, and your son had a hard week and is undeserving of a reward. You have the answers, but you don't have to respond when others try to throw you off course. Instead, pray, breathe, and stay focused.

Keep in mind that answers shouldn't always be offered the moment a question is asked. Sometimes, questions need to be assessed. Maybe you are spoiling your son a bit too much. Maybe you do need to ease up on him just a tad. Maybe the guy you're seeing wouldn't be a good influence on your son. Maybe the golf lessons need to be on hold until you're more financially stable. Maybe it's time to hire that tutor if your son is academically struggling. Maybe new shoes for your son would have been better than buying the dress for yourself. Yeah, questions aren't always meant to harm. Sometimes they are meant to help.

However, you must be willing to receive the question and face the answer head-on. Don't feel pressured by anything or anyone to give an answer right away. Sometimes,

you have to work through, think through, and process information before you can give a response.

I'm not telling you anything you don't know. We realize
all questions aren't bad. We know how to sift through questions and not get flustered by junk.

Sister, you have to teach your son that his life is going
to be filled with questions about many different things.
Those questions are not always going to be what he wants
to hear. Some of them aren't going to be fair either. People
are going to have questions no matter what he does. My
mother taught me that some things in life you just have to
get used to. Teach him to get used to questions.

You should also teach him to always be working through
the answers. Teach him to not give smart-aleck responses,
even when someone is negative to him first. Help him realize how to think through questions so that each one can
make him better.

No question goes unanswered. Your son just needs to
learn to process his way through them all. If you teach him
this, the questions will never overwhelm him, aggravate him,
or frustrate him. Instead, pondering the queries will fuel him
to greatness.

Spiritual Impact

THE STORY OF PETER AND JOHN BEFORE THE SANHEDRIN

(Acts 4:1–7)

As I said earlier, there are a lot of questions in this life; when you know the answers, you are in a better position. Let's tackle the obvious question spurred by this Bible passage first: What is the Sanhedrin? They were the highest religious council of the ancient Jews; they exercised great authority in the Jewish community.

As a single mom, questions probably fill your life in regard to your son: Can you teach him how to be a man? Why do you baby him so much? Would he be better off with his dad? Do you have enough to give him all he needs? Those tough questions can strike a nerve. And if you fully entertain them and are not careful, you may find yourself off track and questioning yourself. The last thing you want to do is get so backed up in a corner with these questions that you begin to question yourself. When you start down this road, it's hard to come back.

But we can learn much from Peter and John. They stood boldly in their position and faced the situation with unshakable strength.

> And as they spake unto the people, the priests, and
> the captain of the temple, and the Sadducees, came
> upon them, being grieved that they taught the people,

and preached through Jesus the resurrection from the dead. And they laid hands on them, and put them in hold unto the next day: for it was now eventide. Howbeit many of them which heard the word believed; and the number of the men was about five thousand. (Acts 4:1–4)

They knew their position *in* Christ and their position *with* Christ. Peter and John stood on the fact that Jesus Christ is the risen Savior.

You have to be sure your position is right as you help your son deal with life's circumstances. Don't question and second guess yourself once you know your decisions and the results of those decisions add up.

And it came to pass on the morrow, that their rulers, and elders, and scribes, and Annas the high priest, and Caiaphas, and John, and Alexander, and as many as were of the kindred of the high priest, were gathered together at Jerusalem. And when they had set them in the midst, they asked, By what power, or by what name, have ye done this? (Acts 4:5–7)

The most important and the most difficult questions you will ever have to deal with will be the ones your son asks. These can cut to the very core of your emotions. Questions like: "Mama, why are you and daddy not together?" "When can I see my dad?" "Why does my father not come around much?" "Why did my dad die?" "How come my father is in jail?" "Did my father want me?"

Questions like these are difficult. Should your son ask any of them one day, you'll address them. When those times come, they can be some of your toughest moments as a mother. But they may also be some of your most courageous moments. You don't want your son to have bitterness or sadness where his father is concerned; so you have to help him through these rough questions.

Let Peter and John be your examples of how to handle this situation. Like them, stand tall and simply speak the truth, regardless how uncomfortable the truth may be. The fact is, no matter the circumstances, your son's father is not with him on a daily basis. Your son needs your answers to help him cope with his reality. Remember you are not alone. The Lord is with you as you help your son. The Word says, "my yoke is easy and my burden is light" (Matthew 11:30). There are no questions too hard for God.

When you press through the tough questions your son will ask, it will be difficult, but the results will all be worth the struggle. If you respond to his questions with truth and forthrightness, he'll learn to face the struggles of life head-on. Your answers can empower him to never run from the hard questions, but to always look for the right answer. He'll go from, "I'm not sure if I can play that sport?" to "Mommy, did you see the winning play I made in the game?" If you respond with honesty to his question, "Why do I have to study so hard to learn?" you may one day hear, "Mom, can you believe I'm Valedictorian?" When he faces defeat, and asks, "Mom, when will I find a job?" your answer can build him up and pave the way for you to one day hear, "Mother, guess what salary they are going to pay me?" Helping your son analyze questions to find the answers he needs to be successful may take work, but will be worth it.

Mama's Story:

THE STORY OF A QUESTIONABLE MOVE

Lesson: You have to know the answers.

Every move you make can be scrutinized by others. Just ask my mother. She bore the weight of ridicule when she decided to move our family across town. Never once did she second guess her decision to get us away from the tough neighborhood to a much better area. Her chief motivation was to get me in a better position of opportunity. I loved the fact that she took into consideration that I could possibly have a better opportunity in one school than I had in another. She also took a lot of criticism for it.

My mother's motto was, "A sacrifice for one is a sacrifice for all." I wasn't the only child; therefore, my brother and sister were affected by moving to another home. And my mother was most definitely affected by the financial aspects of moving her family to a better area. The cost of our new place was almost twice what we had been paying to live in the home we left behind.

People asked many judgmental questions: "Where are you going to get the money?" "Why put yourself in a position to be strapped for cash?" "Can you guarantee that things are going to work out the way you think they will?" One question after another was thrown her way. She might as well have been in a courtroom being interrogated by a harsh, defense attorney. Everyone was in her business! And I felt horrible that she was enduring such tremendous pressure on my behalf. But Mom stayed cool under the scrutiny. I watched her remain unfazed. Staying calm and collected, she addressed everyone's concerns, including mine.

Mom defended her choice to everyone "concerned." She explained that my education wasn't the only reason for the move; the new place was safer, gave Mom greater access to her job, and also put her closer to her sister.

Though I was relieved I wasn't the sole cause of putting more strain on her heart and purse, I still had the same big question as everyone else: "Where are we going to get the money to be able to move?" Now, as badly as I wanted to attend this other school, I certainly did not want my mom to struggle even more trying to pay for this new place. It just wasn't worth it. Turns out, none of us knew my mom was already earning more than we realized. She was only using what she needed, not all of what she had. She maintained that the move meant an overall better situation for us and she was not going to allow all the questions to deter her. When she answered all the questions, everyone was on board with her plan. That situation taught me a great deal about how to field questions.

Using that situation as a teaching opportunity, I remember her telling me that I would be faced with hard decisions as I grew older. She told me not to allow questions from others to change my opinion of what was right for me. I began to realize, if I was to become all I wanted to be, I had to learn how to deal with questions from others.

The questions we face from others in life can be used to stretch our resolve and toughen our character. They can make us better people. To be questioned by others allows us the opportunity to ponder, dismiss, answer, and/or overcome perceived problems or issues seen from those on the outside.

There will always be questions for your son to answer. However, as long as you teach him to have the courage to face them head-on, they will only make him a better man. Let them keep coming!

Athletic Tale

APPALACHIAN STATE'S DEFEAT OF MICHIGAN

Can a small Football Championship Series school beat a heavyweight Football Bowl Subdivision school? Can Appalachian State possibly put in a good showing against powerful University of Michigan? Everyone thought the answer was "No." The questions about App. State's abilities and chances kept coming. For poor little App. State, the questions must have felt like an avalanche of doubt. Good thing the DI-AA school didn't listen to "everyone's" answer.

The lop-sided game started out just the way everyone had thought it would; Michigan took the ball and marched right down the field on a 66-yard score. But as the first quarter continued, App. State returned the favor by scoring on a 68-yard touchdown strike. Michigan went on to score one more time in that first quarter; and by the time the quarter was over, Michigan had a 14 to 7 lead.

Into the second quarter, App. State found a way to tie the game at 14 all.

App. State wasn't done, however; they stopped Michigan on their next possession. After an amazing drive that ended in a touchdown, you could just see the courage mounting for App. State when the scoreboard read 21 to 14 in their favor. App. State got the ball again and scored to make it 28 to 14. Now, everyone began to see that what appeared to be impossible was more than possible. As a matter of fact, they saw it happening right before their eyes. No one had seen this coming! App. St. responded to every question about their ability and then started asking one of their own: "What are you going to do, Michigan, now that you are behind?"

Michigan went on to get three more points before the half ended to cut the score to 29 to 17. As the third quarter started, Michigan got a field goal; but, App. State got it back with a field goal of their own, making the score 31 to 20. Through some wild circumstances, Michigan got the ball back and scored; but they were unsuccessful on a two-point conversion. At the end of the third quarter, the score was 31 to 26, with App. State firmly in the lead. The competitive spirit of this huge underdog was amazing!

After another touchdown, Michigan did go on to take the lead over App. State, 32 to 31. But, App State wasn't done. They got the ball back and capitalized on a field goal to take the lead, making the score 34 to 32. Michigan had one last chance to win the game; but a field goal attempt was blocked and App St. had done the unthinkable—the underdog defeated the powerful foe!

What I like about this story is that it is similar to just what most people think about a single, black mom who has to raise a son on her own. Most people think there is no way she can succeed. The observations made by others can be daunting, if not defeating: "You don't have enough help." "Don't you know that the odds are stacked against you?" "No one believes you can succeed."

Sister, you need to respond to the doubting questions with a statement. Much the same as App. State made a statement to Michigan, letting them know there was no way they would allow the opposing team's questions to cause them to question themselves. You see, sister, it may be a good and healthy thing to flip the script and turn the questions back on your questioners. That's what App. State did.

Just because others may see you as "the underdog" having to raise your son alone, and just because you don't have the assumed strength of a two-parent home, it doesn't mean you are going to lose.

To be completely honest, I know it's easy to get down when you are being questioned about your methods or abilities as a parent. But, when you're questioned, always be ready to respond at the right time. Like App. State, believe in yourself and keep your eyes on that goal. When you begin to see the unbelievable happen because you stuck to it and believed . . . look out!

Sister, let me say this very clearly, you can do the unthinkable and make even the improbable possible. Just as App. State listened to their own inner voice of victory instead of being hindered by the doubts of others, you can lead your son to make that winning touchdown in his own life.

Raise your son to have the courage to answer every question he faces with strength and determination. When people count him out, make sure he counts himself in. When people say he can't, make sure he knows he can. When the world isn't on his side, make sure he knows that, with God on his side, he has the advantage.

If App. St. would have bought in to the negative report of others, they would have failed. But, they answered their critics through their winning actions. Can a small DI-AA school beat a heavyweight D-I school? Yes! Can your son succeed against all odds? Yes! Your son can answer the questions that could hold him back in life in the same way App. State answered their detractors—he can continue to head toward the goal and leave them all in his dust. He must learn to stand up to any and all questions and allow none to discourage him from being who he is or who or what he is capable of becoming. No questions ever have to hold him back!

Inspirational Insight

Stephanie's Message

You know, sister, even as I work on this book with Derrick, I know I'm sick of questions. When will the kids act more appreciative? Why did my television break now? How can I help my family be all they are supposed to be? Why do I feel like I'm not making a difference? Will my career ever take off? Can I get a moment's peace? While I don't know the questions you face, I do share your heart's desire. We just want things better.

Sister, we both have the key. God is the "better" we all need. When we go to Him, we can learn to funnel through life's questions so they don't clog us up.

I hope you enjoyed the encouragement Derrick included in this chapter. Here are three things I pulled out to remember and pass on to my son:

First, *teach him to keep his composure when first questioned*. The one thing I can tell you is if your son loses his composure when questioned, he may provide an answer, but it won't be the best answer. Taking the time to process information is key; particularly because he is still very young and inexperienced. Although there are times when the right response is packaged and ready to go, refusing to respond in haste usually makes the answer better received.

Secondly, *teach him that he doesn't have to be intimidated by the question*. It's the oldest tactic in the book. If he can be intimidated, he will be like prey for his opposition. They will feed off of his fears and take advantage of any opportunity to strike a mighty blow against his pursuit of victory. Your son needs to have a sense of confidence in his answers. If he can be bold enough to display courage in a tough spot, his intimidators will be silenced.

Finally, *teach him to deal with the question*. I don't care how difficult the question, facing it squarely is the key to success. If the question needs to be disregarded, teach him to throw it out. Help him understand that, if the question is warranted, it may help him correct his course. If the question helps him validate his direction, help him learn to use it as encouragement to keep going. The vital point in succeeding is to face each question bravely until he gets to where he needs to be.

As women, it seems we have always been questioned about what we can or can't do. But, I continue to see women overcoming challenges and even stepping up in situations by doing more than is expected. We are there for our children. We give them support. And we give everything to help them make it in this life. We are not leaving or forsaking them! We are here to stay, and it doesn't matter what questions we have to deal with. We will face them and prevail.

When will the kids act more appreciative? They are doing it now; one of them just said, "Thanks." Why did my television break now? Because it was ten years old. Be glad it lasted that long. How can I help my family be all they are supposed to be? Pray and keep working. Why do I feel like I'm not making a difference? Because the devil is busy trying to take you down. Rebuke him. Will my career ever take off? You know you can make a difference, so keep on doing your best. Can I get a moment's peace? No. I can't stop, and you can't stop. Why? **Because you have to raise him, sister!!!**

walking tall

Teach him

how to

overcome

discouragement.

(Taken from Acts 5:27–42)

 Motivational Point

I often remind myself of these eloquent words spoken by the late, great, Dr. Martin Luther King, Jr.: "A man can't ride your back unless it's bent." This tremendous quote from one of the greatest men to ever live is only one of many that have made a difference in my life.

Sister, taking into consideration that I don't know your age, I have to assume that you are at least slightly familiar with the work, history, and civil rights movement led by Dr. King. One of the highest recommendations I make to parents (particularly, African

American parents) is to make certain their child has an educated understanding of who Dr. King was and what he stood for. His nonviolent approach captured the attention, not only of a nation, but of the world. His life wasn't easy, but he stood tall.

To be completely honest (which is the only way to be), his style, attitude, and worldview have served to bring dignity and respect to us, as African Americans. And his wisdom made great strides toward ending the days when we were considered by many to be an inferior people, with few rights, privileges, and opportunities. Sister, the way things were before the wisdom Dr. King spoke to the world is what I call the "slumped-over position." This is why Dr. King's quote fuels me. It makes me aware of the affect perception can have on reception and that attitude can have on outcome.

If you and your son are not in the best of circumstances and have found yourselves in the slumped-over position—a place of discouragement—then it is time for both of you to lift your shoulders, hold your heads up, put those feet in motion, and begin to walk tall.

No doubt, it's not easy to raise him alone; but you're doing it. You might not have all of your wants granted, but your daily bread is all you need. You may not be where you hoped to be in life; but thankfully, your life isn't over. There is something good in every situation if you will allow the

Lord to help you see with His eyes. As a believer, you must find your joy in Him. When you trust the Lord with your circumstances, you will begin to realize you do not walk alone. Sorrow may last for the night, but joy comes in the morning (Ps. 30:5)! With the Lord on your side, you can walk through all things knowing He will work everything to your good (Rom. 8:28). You are more than a conqueror through Him (Rom. 8:37)!

So put off the slumped-over mindset and allow the Lord to renew your mind (Col. 3:10) and give you a positive, hopeful outlook like that of Dr. Martin Luther King, Jr. This positive mindset may start with you. If your son is going to walk tall—overcome peer pressure, resist the urge to cheat, keep himself out of the way of influences that won't lead to success, and steer clear of bad choices that will quickly sideline him—you must champion his efforts and provide a model for him to follow. Lead the way with confidence before your son; live your life with trust and reliance on the power of the Lord.

To walk tall is to be strong and courageous in the face of opposition; it is to respond to life situations with character that is above reproach. Your son is listening to what you say; he's watching what you do and whom you entertain. But mostly, he is observing how you handle issues that life brings your way. Your reactions to these issues are critical. When you're angry, don't let him see you go off. When you're sad, don't let him see you break. When you're frustrated, don't let him see you quit. When things get rough, stop, regroup, breathe, and persevere. More than likely, you can relate to what I'm saying. You've made it this far; so you've probably made great strides toward living a determined, targeted life before your son. Keep it up, sister. Keep standing tall, no matter what.

As your son watches you stand in strength, it will teach him to live the same way. Help him understand that living life based on convictions, core values, and godly principles will provide a sure foundation; when his beliefs are opposed, he will have no doubt about where he stands. If he should ever have to make a choice between drugs or feeling left out of the crew, he will have the strength to walk tall without the crew. If he's ostracized by the "in crowd," he can take pride in the fact that he chose a better way. When the wrong crowd gives him a hard time, he can walk peacefully away knowing he won't have to fear trouble because he stayed away. If ever he should be tempted to cheat on an exam, his strong principles and values will kick in and he'll be proud to do his own work. Even if he fails, he will learn to fail with honor and truth intact. If he should be tempted to steal, he will find the fortitude to flee temptation.

Sister, teach your son to not let anyone or anything ride his back with accusations or pressures to conform to their way of thinking, particularly when they are trying to keep him down. If God wanted his back to be ridden He would have made him a horse. Instead He made him a man. A man is meant to walk tall. Let your son know he has great posture and a nice stride. Convey to him that every word spoken to him that is meant to hurt can become motivation to step his game up to the next level. And as high as the monument for Dr. King now stands in Washington D.C., may your son strive daily to rise to such heights. He may get discouraged along the way, but through your example he'll learn to keep on keepin' on. He'll learn from his mama that he can do anything but give up.

 ## Spiritual Impact

THE STORY OF PETER AND THE APOSTLES GOING ON TRIAL

(Acts 5:27–42)

It seems Peter kept finding himself in one tough situation after another. Mind you, this was not his doing, but came about by the will of God. Confronted with the high priests' orders to refrain from preaching about Jesus, Peter was in a predicament. Since he was under the calling of God to proclaim the gospel, Peter could not obey the law.

You see, sister, when the Lord places something strongly in your heart, no matter how tough the way, you can't quit. God supplies your daily needs; but He placed you here to win souls for Him. He wants you to tell the world about

Him and what He's done. You may often pray to Jesus to do much for you. However, what are you doing for your Savior?

> And when they had brought them, they set them before the council: and the high priest asked them, saying, Did not we straitly command you that ye should not teach in this name? and, behold, ye have filled Jerusalem with your doctrine, and intend to bring this man's blood upon us. Then Peter and the other apostles answered and said, We ought to obey God rather than men. The God of our fathers raised up Jesus, whom ye slew and hanged on a tree. Him hath God exalted with his right hand to be a Prince and a Saviour, for to give repentance to Israel, and forgiveness of sins. And we are his witnesses of these things; and so is also the Holy Ghost, whom God hath given to them that obey him. (Acts 5:27–32)

Peter and the other apostles found themselves in opposition to the authorities of their day. But their answer to their accusers was: "We ought to obey God rather than men," (Acts 5:29). For their boldness, they were arrested and beaten for sharing the gospel with others. Yet, nothing could stop them from doing what the Lord asked of them. No doubt, the apostles fought discouragement and fear— they faced a death sentence, but they stood firm for their Lord. They didn't care about the cost. They refused to give up or give in.

When they heard that, they were cut to the heart, and took counsel to slay them. Then stood there up one in the council, a Pharisee, named Gamaliel, a doctor of the law, had in reputation among all the people, and commanded to put the apostles forth a little space; and said unto them, Ye men of Israel, take heed to yourselves what ye intend to do as touching these men. For before these days rose up Theudas, boasting himself to be somebody; to whom a number of men, about four hundred, joined themselves: who was slain; and all, as many as obeyed him, were scattered, and brought to nought. After this man rose up Judas of Galilee in the days of the taxing, and drew away much people after him: he also perished; and all, even as many as obeyed him, were dispersed. And now I say unto you, refrain from these men, and let them alone: for if this counsel or this work be of men, it will come to nought: but if it be of God, ye cannot overthrow it; lest haply ye be found even to fight against God. And to him they agreed: and when they had called the apostles, and beaten them, they commanded that they should not speak in the name of Jesus, and let them go. And they departed from the presence of the council, rejoicing that they were counted worthy to suffer shame for his name. And daily in the temple, and in every house, they ceased not to teach and preach Jesus Christ. (Acts 5:33–42)

Sister, sometimes you have to stand up for your son and teach him how and when to stand tall for himself or for what he believes. Sometimes, the pressure can seem overwhelming; but you have to keep in mind that walking tall when the pressure is at its worst is when courage and determination can most clearly be seen. No one can see you when your back is bent—when you are bowed low from a load of care, inadequacy, or fear.

In the passage of Scripture we read earlier, Gamaliel, an honored Pharisee and a teacher of the law, stood up in a formal meeting of all religious leaders, the Sanhedrin. Each person in the room carried incredible power and influence. Gamaliel ordered that the apostles be taken aside; then he addressed the Sanhedrin. Gamaliel said, "Refrain from these men, and let them alone: for if this counsel or this work be of men, it will come to nought" (Acts 5:38). He clearly warned that attempting to silence the apostles and to force them to relinquish their beliefs and to turn from their convictions could actually place the Sanhedrin in opposition to God. Gamaliel knew his speech could have led to a bad end—for himself as well as the apostles. Yet he stood tall and did what he knew to be right (Acts 5:39).

Peter and the apostles were subsequently released, having never wavered from their strong stand for the Lord. They went on to proclaim the good news of Jesus Christ to all who would listen. Under much opposition, these men kept walking tall and ultimately accomplished their mission to go and tell the world about Jesus, the Messiah (Mark 16:15).

Peter and the apostles stood strongly on their faith and Gamaliel's stance followed suit. When you stand tall, others are drawn to your courage and will walk tall with you. God sends people to see you through, to speak on your behalf, and to lend a hand.

Sister, the only thing that matters when striving to achieve greatness is the mission, not the madness that may come up in your life or in your son's life. Therefore, you have to walk tall right through anything that threatens to get either of you off course. Finances, illness, job issues, any number of life's pressures could be standing in your way. Your son may face bullies, academic challenges, or negative influences. The face of the madness you and your son encounter may change; but it is inevitable that some threat will rise up against you. At those times, you have to stand up, dig deep, and get things done; you must rise to all challenges. Begin teaching your son as early as possible to stand up for what's right. He should be taught to speak up against injustice. He needs to know it's okay to go against the grain, when the grain is wrong according to the final authority—the Word of God.

We all want our sons to be victorious when they are faced with violent opposition. We pray they experience the same kind of outcome against their opponents that Peter and the Apostles enjoyed. Imagine! Peter knew he could be killed if he didn't give in. Yet, he stayed composed and true to God. He had faith. That faith gave him the power to hold his ground. The Lord stepped in and gave Peter help to get out of a dangerous situation.

When you stand with Jesus, you can't be stopped! Sister; tell your son this truth! I pray he has accepted Christ. If so, I can already see his chest rising and his head held high . . . proud that he walks with God.

Mama's Story:

THE STORY OF FOOD STAMPS

Lesson: Be proud, but not prideful.

Here is what I can tell you about the woman who raised me: she was astounding! I have no idea how she managed to raise her family on the meager funds available to her. The only answer is that Emmanuel God was with her. Every time I think about the many desperate situations she led us through, I am amazed! The feats she managed to pull off were downright incredible.

As a single mother of three, equipped with few resources and sparse opportunities, my mom's advantages were few and far between. Even if you've never experienced it, you can imagine living in poverty isn't easy. But, as my mother can tell you, having no husband in the home, no degree behind her, and no family money to depend on, made raising me and my siblings even more challenging.

Mom felt discouraged many days, over many things, as she struggled to raise her kids. Depression threatened when she couldn't take us on summer vacations. She was disheartened at the start of each school year when she was unable to buy us new clothes. She was dispirited when Christmas presents for her kids were few and far between. There were so many things she wanted to do for her children, but could not. That real fact weighed heavily on her heart; but Mom could not and would not wallow in sorrow over what might have been. She had a job to do; and she was determined get us through, using whatever she had. She was always resourceful. She found creative ways to get us what we needed. While she didn't like having to ask for help, she got over her aversion and did what she had to do.

I will never forget one specific situation. Much to my mother's regret, we had to live with the assistance of food stamps for a time. Now, to know my mother is to know a proud, tough, and courageous person. If you think my mother *wanted* to be on food stamps, you'd be utterly wrong. There was no way she would have chosen to be the recipient of welfare. However, she was wise enough to know the help was necessary for a period of time. You see, my mother knew she could walk; she just suffered a bit of a sideline by life and needed crutches to help her along the way for a while. She wasn't so prideful that she would allow her family to go hungry; but she had enough pride to strengthen her legs, so she could walk on her own as soon as possible. Make no mistake, food stamps or not, she always knew the art of walking tall.

I guess her example is where I got my temperament for football. I can assure you, on a football field, you better be confident, strong, and brave. And being prideful is a sure way for a *former* football player to find himself looking down on the grid iron from the stands.

TIME OUT!

Early on, my mother taught me the difference
between having pride and being prideful: Pride
says, "If I can do it on my own, I will; but when I
recognize I need help, I'll accept it." Being prideful
creates one major difference. Prideful people won't
ask for help. They would rather suffer, and let
those around them suffer as well, than ever admit
they can't do all things alone. This attitude is one
of arrogance and egotism—a volatile pairing that
will ultimately lead to destruction.

Sister, I admire you for your tenacity. The daily task to
take care of your family alone is daunting; yet, regardless of
what pulls at your spirit, you find a way. However, even with
your best intentions, life sometimes conspires to create situations you simply can't handle alone. At those times, you
have to weigh your options and consider what's best for all
those who depend on you. Keep your eyes on the purpose
of your actions, not on whatever embarrassment you may
feel. What matters is that your son gets fed, has a roof over
his head, has clothes on his back, has a good education, has
a loving mother, and has Jesus in his heart.

Discouragements will come. Your son probably already
knows everything he wants will not come his way. However,

teaching him to hold on to his pride through the trials of life will help him receive the lessons life has to impart. It's possible for him to hold on so tight to his own pride that no one can take anything out of his hand, and no one can put anything in it. Pride must be kept in balance, just as other aspects of life with the Lord are to be balanced by Him. Healthy pride allowed to run rampant becomes a prideful, arrogant, egotistical attitude that overtakes a heart. And that is certainly not what you want to teach him. Help your son understand, as my mother taught us, there is a huge difference between wants and needs. When wants go wanting, no one is really any worse for wear; unrealized wants can only disappoint us. But unrealized needs can disrupt our lives. If pride stops us from accepting help to supply needs, it has crossed over into the self-important realm of a prideful heart. Prideful behavior gets in the way for so many folks. Don't let it get in your way. My mother use to say: I hate I'm in this mess. But I am not worried about what other people think of me or about what I have to do to get us out of the mess. I am doing what I need to do, not necessarily what I want to do. As long my actions and decisions are honest, legal, and morally sound, I have no problem with my choices and no one else should.

Sister, your son will come to a point in the road when he can't have what he wants; but what he *can* get will sustain him. Please teach him that a bird in the hand always beats two in a bush. Remind him that he has you, teachers, administrators, preachers, mentors, coaches, family, and other positive folks who can help when tough times come. He doesn't have to stay down; he is capable of walking tall.

Tell him the same thing my mom told me when needing assistance caused me to get discouraged: Boy, you're bummed we're on food stamps. Be thankful you're eating! You better pick your head up, pull your shoulders back, grab a smile, put one foot in front of the other, walk tall to the counter, and hand the clerk those food stamps. Be grateful we have something to pay with. And work hard in life so one day you won't need any.

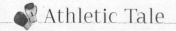 Athletic Tale

THE STORY OF HOW MANY PEOPLE COUNTED AN OLD BOXER OUT

In November of 1994, George Foreman became the oldest boxer in history to become the World Heavyweight Champion. George was forty-five years old and no one believed this ex-heavyweight champ could come out of retirement and recapture the title. No one, that is, except George. I mean, let's be real! How could a man who was forty-five years old do something that people almost half his age struggled to do?

You might be able to understand the criticism. It came from everywhere: "You're too old for a comeback!" "Your reflexes are too slow!" "It's too late for you." Words like these could easily have discouraged George; at the very least, they probably made him think twice about his comeback attempt. Thankfully, George would not let the critics get him down. He was not about to allow what others said turn him back from his dreams. The media kept reporting the fact that Michael Moorer, his challenger and the holder of the heavyweight title, was nineteen years younger than big George. They even went on to say that there was little risk involved for Moorer; although he had to take Foreman seriously, he need not worry about losing the fight.

You see, sister, just when the world says you can't raise your son to be a successful, young, black man, you get ready to prove them wrong. Sister, when everybody takes the side of the pessimist about your situation, discouragement can easily find its way to your doorstep. Doom and gloom can bend you over. Many sometimes count us out before we begin. Even really looking at what lies ahead sometimes can be hard to face. In the times when the mountain looks too high to climb, climb anyway.

Despite the odds, George kept his back straight and walked tall into battle. On November 5, 1994, George foreman fought Michael Moorer in front of a packed house in Las Vegas, Nevada. From the opening bell, Michael began proving that age does matter in boxing. Moorer punished George for nine rounds, and it looked bad for the former heavyweight champion. One of the things that fascinated me about big George Foreman was after each round he would retreat to his corner, but he remained standing until the bell would ring to resume the match. How could a middle-aged man fail to take the opportunity to sit and recover?

As the fight continued and Foreman struggled, the expected outcome seemed inevitable. Then it happened! In the tenth round, Foreman caught Moorer with a right hand to the face; with a lacerated mouth, Moorer fell to the canvas. The referee's count began. Moorer could not regain his feet. The impossible had happened: George Foreman won the battle and recaptured the title of Heavyweight Champion of the world!

A good portion of the world is infamous for overlooking our accomplishments while making us feel as if we don't belong. The critics claimed loudly that George did not belong in a "young man's sport." But George changed their minds when he answered the bell in the tenth round that November night. Sister, there is much you can learn from George Foreman's tenacity; and the spirit of Foreman's effort can help you teach your son that success will often take place right in the middle of a lot of discouraging circumstances.

Take a look at your own life. You're in your own ring of battle, fighting through tough circumstances. You know what I'm saying? You have to knock the bills out, dance around your schedule to get it all done, punch that clock daily so you can get a paycheck. You are fighting and you are winning. Teach your son to do the same. Make sure he knows to block everything around him out and go to work with the idea that he is one punch away from victory. George Foremen beat the odds because he stood tall when backed into a corner, yet came out swinging hard. Your son can be a champion, too. Ding, ding!

Inspirational Insight
Stephanie's Message

The message of this chapter was right on time for me! Honestly, this morning, I'm discouraged. My father ran for the local school board. Last night the results came in. Though he has tons of credentials, campaigned extensively, and has a heart for the kids, he was defeated. Seeing my father disappointed tears at my heart, and I just want to find a way to ease his pain. What happens when you can't reverse the outcomes, or can't get rid of the cancer, or can't bring a loved one back? You get discouraged.

My father told me he'll be okay. He can still serve, give, and help. My dad is still teaching me, even though I'm a grown woman. He showed me that, though we get discouraged when things we want don't come our way, we don't have to live defeated. It's natural to feel down sometimes when you go through hard times or when someone you love deals with something difficult. However, because we're like Peter and the apostles and know Jesus, we must stand tall.

This chapter motivated me to help my son, who is a senior in high school, walk tall. Here are three things I gleaned from this chapter. I hope Derrick's insights will help you help your son walk tall, as well.

First, *teach him to not buy into the "I can't" way of thinking*. Derrick lives by a winning creed; he is always saying: If you think you dare not, you don't. If you like to win and think you can't, it's almost a cinch you won't. If you think you'll lose, then you've already lost. For out in the world you'll find that success begins with a person's will. It's all in their state of mind. If you think you are out-classed, then you are. You have to think high and rise before you can ever win a prize. Life's battles don't always go to the stronger or faster man; but the one who wins is the one who thinks he can. Come what may in your son's life, teach him to look at it from the positive.

Secondly, *teach him to not buy into the "I wish" mentality*. A lot of people live wishing they had this or that.

Well sister, if your son is ever going to rise to the top, you need to make sure you teach him not to *wish* for what he wants but to set his will in motion toward what he wants. This is something Derrick is always talking about. Don't ever underestimate the power of the human will. Derrick believes if the will to achieve is strong enough, it will happen; and if it doesn't happen, then accept God's will and move on. Sister, don't let your son *wish* his way through life; teach him to *work*.

Finally, *teach him to not buy into the "somebody else will do it" mentality*. That's right! You have to make sure he understands if anything is going to get done, he is going to have to do it. People help those who help themselves. Sister, model this for him as you work toward your goals. Don't coddle your son and allow him to sit idly wishing his life away. Challenge him! Enable him to live up to expectations by encouraging him; even in things as simple as requiring him to pick up his own things instead of depending on someone else to do his work for him.

My mind keeps going back to my father and the race he didn't win; it's still unsettling. (Cut me slack! He just lost last night.) It hurts. It feels yucky. It is no fun seeing my dad on the losing end. But I have to give it to him, he tried. He wanted something, and he went after it. He felt a calling to run; and regardless of the outcome, he gave his all.

Reading the passage from Scripture Derrick highlighted here, I learned from Peter's story that when we stand for what is right and good, God will help us stand tall. I saw my dad living this out last night. He was gracious in defeat. He congratulated his opponent. He talked positively to reporters, and he told me God has something better for him. Wow! Sister, isn't that the way you want your son to think?

Let's teach our sons to stand tall when discouragement comes, and they want to lie down and quit. Let's teach them to fall on their knees, instead. We can help them keep moving, keep going, and keep walking tall. Our sons can be victors; but not because they get everything they want. They can be victors in Christ because, regardless of what comes, they can live as overcomers. **Raise him, sister!!!**

no limitations

Teach

him to

never stop.

(Taken from Acts 9:36–43)

Motivational Point

"The sky is the limit!" "Reach for the stars!" "You can do anything you put your mind to!" These are phrases that motivate us to strive for the impossible and accomplish the incredible. They speak of a hope for success that pushes us through difficulties, and a love for a dream that helps us remain relentless until we apprehend it. Honestly, it is hard to rise to this level, but when we do, we are never the same.

Sister, you know your son has the potential to achieve great things. Put no limitations on yourself or him as you help him rise from the place he is to the place he wants to be. You can be the agent of influence who encourages him toward limitless thinking. It will take this kind of internal wherewithal to push past mediocrity and achieve the astonishing.

I can see you doing the small, daily things that push you beyond what seems difficult. You're exhausted, but you keep going. You need more qualifications; you go get them. Your son is frustrating you, but you don't give up on him. Yes, sister, these examples are a mere few of how you possibly push yourself to never settle, even when settling, giving in, and giving up is easier. You are a mom on a mission, determined to push past barriers and obstacles. You will accept no supposed "limitations" as being insurmountable. You have set your course to be the best you can be and to raise a successful young man.

Limitations can come wrapped in so many packages. Often, the limitations in our way are the ones we have imposed on ourselves. Sometimes, we have to get out of our own way—move those limitations, and create an environment of infinite potential. Take a moment and consider the things you regard as limitations. What are the things that hinder your progress in life and affect your ability to help your son progress toward his future success? Put together a short list of the limitations you see. After you acknowledge the obstacles, your task is to face each one squarely and with courage. As your son sees you confronting any obstacles and determining to find a way to reach beyond them, he will begin to see each obstruction in his path as a challenge to be overcome. Limitations can actually become tools that create real fortitude in him.

I recognize that, as a single woman, you may face limitations and real challenges that make raising your son more complicated, especially at particular turns in his journey. The fact that you are not a man doesn't mean you can't and won't raise him to be an awesome male. Let's talk real, though. At some point, your son may feel he is getting too big for his britches and may begin to think you have nothing to teach him. You and he may both feel that only a man can teach him how to be a man. When he gets bigger and stronger, he may try you. A father may have been able to face him down physically; but, sister, there are other ways to put your grown son in his place. I challenge you to not let his size or bulk get in the way of enforcing firm expectations; don't let physical attributes inhibit your ability to connect with your son. This is one area where you need to break through the limitations and find a way to be the parent he needs.

Your son already understands that you are a caring, loving, supportive mother. But when he comes to grips with the fact that you are also the firm disciplinarian who demands respect on every level and in all situations, he will then begin to respect you and never consider what he may be missing by having a father in his life. This is not to suggest that the absence of a father figure is the ideal you would choose for him; instead, your son won't feel the lack if you step up and be a strong woman of God. Never forget that when God calls, He enables. He will give you all you need to parent your son in such a way that he will see and understand what he needs to be for his own family one day. The lessons you teach him can inform his understanding of the roles two parents should play. You can help him understand that sharing the load is vital to a successful family unit. Being a single mom is a limitation only if you allow it to be. Step up and take hold of the enabling power the Lord will give you. By doing so, you will go far toward teaching him that there are no limitations that can't be overcome . . . if he wants to overcome them badly enough.

In my own life, every time a limitation presents itself, I rely on my faith. The Word says if we have the faith of a mustard seed, mountains can be moved (Matt. 17:20). We must grab hold of our faith when we face adversity. We've got to believe we can cross any river. We have to know we can climb out of any valley. We must not stop dreaming, trying, and striving until we are standing on top of any obstacle in our paths. God is there to see us through. Our faith in Him and His will for our lives removes the doubt caused by anything that stands in our way.

Sister, your son needs to know this. Teach him that any limitation that threatens to stop him can be a powerful opportunity for operating in faith. Obstacles can propel him to face challenges head on, dig deep when it gets hard, and never stop until he accomplishes his goals. This is another place to lead by example. Remember, you are the strong presence in your son's life. Go ahead! Tell those limitations you jotted down to get out of your way. The more loudly and confidently you confront them, the more definitely your son will hear you; and he may just gain the same confident faith. Soon he'll tell his limitations to get out of his way, too. Won't it be a proud day when limitless thinking is one of his best friends?

 ## Spiritual Impact

THE STORY OF PETER BRINGING A DEAD WOMAN TO LIFE

(Acts 9:36–43)

Can there be any greater limitation placed on someone than to be overtaken by death? Death is supposed to be the end—time to say our goodbyes, lower the casket, and move on. As much as we may desire it, we can't bring the dead back to life. Right?

The people of Joppa were at this very place as our story begins. It seemed all that could be done was to take Tabitha's body and place it in the ground. But, Peter had been given a powerful, overcoming faith by Almighty God. By that faith, Peter was able to reach beyond human limitation.

TIME OUT!

Now there was at Joppa a certain disciple
named Tabitha, which by interpretation is
called Dorcas: this woman was full of good
works and almsdeeds which she did. (Acts
9:36)

I can't resist highlighting the character traits
Tabitha possessed. She was quite a woman and the
reports given about her are really impressive.

Every chance you get to talk to your son about
character, please do so. A godly character is
always impressive; and a negative, problematic
character carries an impact of its own. People will
notice his behavior either way. Isn't it best to make
sure he does his part to be known for positive
things?

And it came to pass in those days, that she was sick,
and died: whom when they had washed, they laid her
in an upper chamber. And forasmuch as Lydda was
nigh to Joppa, and the disciples had heard that Peter
was there, they sent unto him two men, desiring him
that he would not delay to come to them. Then Peter
arose and went with them. When he was come, they
brought him into the upper chamber: and all the widows stood by him weeping, and shewing the coats

and garments which Dorcas made, while she was with
them. But Peter put them all forth, and kneeled down,
and prayed. (Acts 9:37–40)

Obviously, when Peter arrived on the scene, everyone
was in mourning for their dear, departed friend. So Peter
wasted no time—he immediately dropped to his knees in
prayer.

Prayer is a secret to success that so many people don't
access. When we give our problems to the Lord, He provides clarity, direction, and answers. God wants to send
forth His power to change any situation into a blessing for
us. We just have to take our issues to Him. Please teach
your son the value of prayer.

Notice that before Peter prayed, he sent the mourn-
ers from the room. Scripture doesn't tell us the reason
Peter cleared the room; but I wonder if maybe he wanted
those who could not believe in a miracle to leave the scene.
Maybe their doubt would have hampered the miracle that
was about to take place.

Regardless, there is no doubt that pessimistic people who lack faith can have a negative impact on everyone
around. Make sure you keep people around you and your
son who believe in his future and want the best for him.
These are the people who will pray for you and rejoice with
you when they hear about your son's achievements and his
success at pressing beyond any limitations.

. . . and turning him to the body said, Tabitha, arise. And
she opened her eyes: and when she saw Peter, she sat
up. And he gave her his hand, and lifted her up, and
when he had called the saints and widows, presented
her alive. And it was known throughout all Joppa; and
many believed in the Lord. And it came to pass, that
he tarried many days in Joppa with one Simon a tan-
ner. (Acts 9:40–43)

After the miracle took place, many people were won to
the Lord. Peter saw the power of God working through him
and watched as an entire town was impacted by his faithful-
ness to his God-given purpose.

Sister, your son's life will definitely hold situations and
circumstances that seem daunting; but help him understand he need not be limited by them. Help him learn to
look beyond what he can see into what can be. Sometimes,
there is more than one way to get things done. Teach your
son to search for alternate routes toward his dream when
limitations attempt to push him backward. His limitations
will grow larger if he suffers from a lack of desire to locate
another avenue to move him forward. Limitations disappear
when determination and faith combine to create an alternate path.

In a previous chapter, I mentioned how much I appreciate my former Special Teams Coach, Frank Gansz. Often,
when his team was presented with limitations, he would say,
"You have to learn to midstream adjust." When he put it

that way, we got it. If you can't go right, go left. If you can't go around, jump over. When there is a wall, knock it down.

As you teach your son to face down the obstacles, make sure you help him understand clearly that God can make a way where there is no way. Tell him: When you feel there is no more hope and your situation is dead, don't count God out. Let the Holy Spirit living inside you guide you to make adjustments. Learning to modify plans is a necessary art if you wish to follow where the Lord leads. Let Him direct your path, and your destination will exceed your fondest dreams.

When faced with seemingly crippling limitations, both you and your son should remember Peter and how he responded in a situation that seemed hopeless. He saw the ultimate limitation as Tabitha's death stared him in the face; yet he did not accept that it was a hopeless situation. He turned to the source of all hope and did as His God inspired him to do. He allowed God to lead him onto an alternate path—a path that held life in place of death, hope in place of despair, and victory in the place of defeat.

Be inspired by Peter. Be willing to find other ways to arrive at your desired destination. When you have a burning desire to accomplish anything great, nothing can stop you. Don't cry and pout when faced with adversity, remember Peter's story and be ready to rise to the occasion. Teach your son to embrace an altered route to his dreams by thinking outside the box. Let him know that the only "box" that can keep him confined is the one in which he places himself.

So, two important questions arise when facing limitations in life: How much do you want greatness for your son? How much does he want it for himself? I believe the answers are found in how hard you both are willing to PUSH!

Mama's Story:

THE STORY OF HAVING LIMITATIONS, BUT NOT BEING LIMITED

Lesson: There is a way.

Can I make it perfectly clear about the value of an education? Education is money. No one pays someone who knows nothing. If you don't know how to flip a hamburger, the fast food joint says, "bye." If you can't count money, the bank says, "Sorry, you aren't qualified." If you didn't get a degree, the school system can't have you teaching kids what you don't know. My mom told me early that she wished she'd gotten more of an education, so she would have had more opportunities. As a parent, I now fully understand why it was so important to her that I get an education. She wanted me to push further than she did. Sound familiar?

There is nothing more necessary or more capable of providing the tools required to succeed in what is a very competitive world than the knowledge acquired from books. We spend so much time preaching to our children about the importance of getting an education. We say, "Make sure you do your homework." "Don't forget to turn your project in." "Are you ready for the test on Friday?" These are just a few of the many reminders we, as parents, are always repeating in some form.

One of the reasons I find my mother's story so amazing is what she accomplished with so little. You see, she was a woman who refused to allow her limited academic knowledge get in the way of her son's academic and future success. She had no formal, higher education; but she learned whatever she needed to know about being a successful mother.

Even though Mom didn't have a college degree, she was one wise lady. Though she never studied college English, she spoke with sound grammar that never failed to make her meaning clear. Never once did I fail to understand her communication of do's and don'ts. In the area of math, Mom excelled in grasping the value of a dollar. She could count pennies with the best of them. Her perception of science was over the top. No one could pull together more effective concoctions or potions; whether she was formulating meals or cures, Mom surpassed all learned scientists when it came to raising well-fed, healthy kids. Watching all of her knowledge and wisdom unfold right before my very eyes, each and every day, was something to see!

I remember one particular day when I was giving Mom drama at home. I was an arrogant tenth grader, sure I was fully grown, and Mom didn't like me bucking up my chest at her. She was on me about my grades, and I smarted off about her education. She said some words that went in one of my ears and out the other. I smacked my lips and considered the matter closed when she stormed away.

When I got to school the next morning, I learned she had been working on my behalf, even when I didn't know it, to get me the help I needed to set me straight. You see, I had a tough, strong football coach whom I respected. My mother talked to him, and he got on to me. Let's just say, what he said and how he said it, sunk in. I never disrespected or belittled my mother *ever* again.

Looking back, I love how she played her hand. I was getting bigger, so I thought I had the upper hand. I pointed out her lack of education, so I considered myself above her. I was going down the wrong road with my nasty attitude, so I had her frustrated. However, where she was limited by circumstances beyond her control, she got help to straighten me out. She found someone bigger than me, physically, to keep me in check. She got someone who had a college degree to call me out, so I couldn't talk junk about education. And she found someone who could handle my attitude with no problem. When coach was done with me, my mom had reached beyond her limitations to accomplish what she couldn't on her own. In the end, she definitely got through to me.

Mom told me that when she didn't know what to do, she turned to the Best Teacher. She loved sitting in the classroom of God. She said all of her learning came from Him. She believed that where she was limited, He was limitless. Therefore, in the area of education, she enjoyed the "Master's Degree" from Him. My mother truly believed in the Bible and in its power to not only change a life, but to direct a life. She discovered the Bible is a great source for wisdom regarding daily living. From the pages of God's Word, Mom learned how to talk to people, how to count the cost with every choice that she made, and how to impact a situation through the ways in which she was gifted. Sister, she knew the secret to having no limitations.

You may sometimes feel you are limited in what you can do for your son. But God has promised to supply all of our needs (Phil. 4:19); so you will never lack in what your son needs from you.

Can you imagine all the areas of your son's life in which God wants to prove Himself limitless? Can you even dream all the places our Lord wants to take your young man? How many lives will he touch? What is the work the Lord has prepared for him (Eph. 2:10)?

Sister, take the time to teach your son that there is a way to greatness that is right and rewarding. Help him understand there are no limitations that are insurmountable in his pursuit of being everything the Lord has called him to be. And like my mother, call in reinforcements when they're needed. Do whatever it takes to take your son beyond any limitations.

 ## Athletic Tale

THE STORY OF TEAM HOYT

I would like to introduce to you the father and son tandem, Dick and Rick Hoyt—Team Hoyt, as they are so inspirationally called. Dick and his son, Rick, compete together in marathons and triathlons across the country. This is no ordinary story; nor are these ordinary people. There is a better word to describe Dick and Rick Hoyt: EXTRAORDINARY!

Team Hoyt knows the true meaning of overcoming limitations—the team is made up of a father beyond his prime and a son who is confined to a wheel chair. If there were such a thing as an ultimate limitation in the world of sports, being severely, physically handicapped would certainly

TIME OUT!

You might not be aware of the grueling aspects of a triathlon. In most cases, Triathlons consist of three athletically challenging events: swimming 0.93 miles, cycling 24.8 miles, and running 6.2 miles. Under normal circumstances, these triathlon feats are accomplished by a single individual.

qualify. No exceptions or allowances are made in a triathlon to accommodate such handicaps. But, as it turns out, this father and son team refused to accept a "handicapped" designation. If there were pictures that capture the meaning and spirit of "pushing" your son to win, seeing this team in motion would qualify as the most striking. Against all odds and without claiming any special considerations for the obstacles they face, Rick and Dick Hoyt face the challenges and finish the races. The 2009 Boston Marathon marked Rick and Dick Hoyt's 1,000th race.

It is an interesting twist that Dick feels he is being pushed by his son, Rick. It is the love and care this father has for his son that drives him. But what inspires Dick the most is that Rick, though wheelchair bound, wants to compete more than his father. Seemingly limited by his so-called handicap to a life without athletic competition, Rick refuses to allow a wheelchair to prevent him from doing what he really wants to do. Rick wants to run. He wants to cycle. He wants to swim. And, with his dad doing whatever is necessary to make that happen, Rick does all three. Though Rick must deal with clear and obvious limitations, what is on the inside of this unlikely athlete is something I wish every kid in the world could have. Rick has passion and desire enough to cause him to reach beyond all obstacles and use his limitations as opportunities to succeed.

You see, sister, to overcome barriers you must desire to achieve; but what motivates you must not just come from the mind only. To overcome barriers and leave limitations in your dust, the motivation must also flow from the most important places of all—your heart and soul.

Your son may have what appear to be limitations placed on him. He may not be happy his dad isn't around. He may not be the smartest. He may not be the fastest. He may not be the richest. He may not have all he wants. So what? Some have it worse. Even the worst poverty in America pales in comparison to the dire conditions suffered by so many in third-world countries. Whatever the limitation, there is a reason to be thankful and a way to turn a seeming disadvantage into a step toward achievement. What your son must do when confronted by obstacles is find a way around, through, over, or under. Help him learn to view any limitation as a challenge to be accepted and overcome. He may need help; he may even require God's miraculous intervention. But, remember, when God calls, He enables. If God wants your son to achieve, nothing on the face of the earth can stand in your son's way but your son.

Rick Hoyt, in so many ways, is proclaiming from his wheel chair that he will not allow any limitation to stand in his way. In his heart and soul he wanted to find a way to excel in life. He could not physically swim, but his father could. He could not physically run, but his father could. And he could not physically cycle, but his father could. So Dick Hoyt became the legs and arms that carry his son toward his dream.

Sister, your son may not have such visible challenges. He may not have limitations that cause physical restrictions. But your son will face limitations and challenges of his own. And when he does, he will need you to move him along in the right way. When your son is not able to go it on his own, remember Team Hoyt and push him until he crosses that finish line.

Inspirational Insight
Stephanie's Message

Wow! Another of Derrick's chapters was right on time with exactly what I needed! You see, I've been so frustrated with my son's lack of enthusiasm. He's a senior in high school and, honestly, some days I'd like to see a lot more "get up and go" from him. Earlier today, I asked my son to do something, and he laid there and mumbled. He was getting in his own way. He needed me to set him straight, but he was not ready for my response. I'd read this chapter, and I was inspired. Like Peter, I prayed and then told my son something I honestly can't remember. However, I can remember that I said it with such force, conviction, and power that he could only get up and get going.

Limitations are designed to stop us or, at least, plant the suggestion that we should stop. They can cause us to give up on what we really want to do in life. They can be our greatest obstacles to experiencing the abundant life God wants to give us. With that in mind, let me give you three ways to help your son press through and find a way around any limitations—even those limitations he places on himself.

First, *teach him to not settle for a limited life*. Girl, let's face it, nobody wants to be limited. However, we all have limitations. The secret is finding ways around those limitations through creative thinking. Who would not want everything to go as planned or unfold the way they desire? But the hard reality is that it seldom happens that way. So when those limitations are placed on your son, help him get creative with a solution. Help him reach deep inside and find the resolve to say he won't be stopped.

Secondly, *teach him that developing his resolve is paramount*. Determination, steadfastness, and tenacity are all character traits of a person who possesses resolve. Your son needs to learn that the one who truly wins is the one who endures to the end. He needs to find a way. He needs to learn to fight on without all the stuff he thinks he needs. He needs to be ready to stay in the game.

Derrick is always talking about resolve. He says resolve is the kind of mindset that takes limitations and stretches them until there are no limits. I was moved by the Hoyt's story. Rick was given many physical limitations, yet he has done so much in spite of them.

So what if your son has limitations placed on him? He's got you to push him beyond his limitations. And ultimately, he'll develop the resolve to push himself.

Finally, *teach him to always be ready to show others what he is made of*. In so many cases, the best opportunity to do this is "when push comes to shove." You know, when things are tough at home, on the job, or with people, when there seems to be one problem after another, mothers don't cave . . . we attack! Being counted out, or being told we can't or won't, can cause us to give in to defeat. However, with the Lord on our side and with determination in our hearts, we tread on anyway, proving people wrong and making ourselves proud.

Our sons may not be there yet. I know mine is still somewhat immature. Oh well, time for me to grow him up so he can show people he has what it takes. I know how hard it is to keep trying to find a way when obstacles continue to get in the way. Everywhere you turn there are more bills, more attitudes, and more drama. How can you keep your head above water? How can you not give in? How can you will yourself to pray, obey, and rise? And when you're dealing with so much, it can be difficult to focus on your son and give him the help he needs.

Well, dear sister, when you feel the walls closing in, don't you ever stop pushing. Life might not be fair sometimes (for you or your son). You may be facing a father who is absent, a job that was lost, or "no help, nowhere . . . ever." In times like these, remember the good news: God is with you, and He can't be limited . . . not His love and not His power. So no matter what it is, girl, don't set your eyes on the limitations; instead, focus on the Lord and ask His help in finding a way around any obstacles in your path. Even when it gets rough, tough, hard, and you've faced enough stuff, you better not stop **praising God and raising your son up!!!**

CHAPTER *6*

crystal
clear

Teach

him to

think he can

do it too.

(Taken from Acts 11:1–18)

 ## Motivational Point

Imagine it's a hot day, and you want something to cool your thirst. You may want sweet tea, lemonade, Coca-Cola, water, or some other refreshing drink. No matter what you choose, chances are, you'll drink it from a glass. Whether you're at your home, someone else's place, or at a restaurant, you want your glass to be sparking clean. You deserve to drink from a clean glass. You have no desire to get germs by drinking from a dirty glass. Even if you have to rewash a glass for yourself, you will, because it must be sparkling clean.

Well, the way you want to raise your son is much the same. Just as you want a clean glass, you want your son to be spotless. Just as you would choose a glass with no left-over food in it, you want your son to not be left out of opportunities. You would choose a glass with no smudges, just as you don't want your son to have any smudges on his character, real or imagined, because his dad isn't around. You choose a glass with no dishwasher residue; in the same way you don't want your son to miss out on chances because of the color of his skin. You want the world to look at your son in the same way they would look at the perfect glass in the cabinet. You want them to choose him because he is perfect.

TIME OUT!

As you are aware, no one is perfect. Only our Lord and Savior, Jesus Christ, is perfect. We cannot know the perfection of our Lord while we live on this earth, but there is nothing wrong with striving to be the absolute best we can be.

In most areas of life, it is imperative that we strive for as much perfection as we can gain. In some areas, we must convey clearly where we stand and leave no doubt in anyone's mind. Important aspects of life demand that we make our intentions crystal clear. Things others don't consider worth the effort, if we know them to be our duty, we must see as obligations.

Sister, your son is your obligation. No matter what anyone else may think, he is important and, after the Lord, should be the top priority in your life. He deserves the opportunity for success and significance just as much as those who may have more, or who have had the experience of having a father present. He is no less deserving of the commitment of time, resources, and support just because you have to serve as the primary care giver. As a matter of fact, he is going to be more in need of all you can give. Here's a principle you want to teach him: when you have less, you must give more.

It could be that your son wants to participate in sports, but others have more talent than he does. This is no excuse to quit. Your son has to work harder and do more. Lack of natural talent doesn't mean he can't play on the team. It means he has to find a way to utilize what he has and develop what he does not have. Encourage him to work and make sure he understands he has as much right to success as the next person. This is a message he must grasp as early as possible. Don't allow your son to accept an inferiority complex because of his perception of who he is, or who he isn't.

Communicating the importance of a positive self-image as you interact with him on a daily basis is paramount. It's important that you serve as the catalyst for his acceptance of his own self-worth. Make sure he knows that he belongs at the table and that there is a seat just for him. Teach him his self-worth is not dependent upon how much he has to learn. Help him understand that his value is a constant, even as he continues to reinvest in his development.

Everyone has value that others would and should consider worth the effort. But for your son, the impact of your approval will transcend everyone's opinion. The more your son recognizes the value you place on him, the greater the value he will place on himself. If you show him the real value of his existence through the way you pour into his life, no one will be able to diminish his own perceived self-value. If you teach him to value himself while he is young, it can give your son the self-esteem he needs to appreciate who he is and strive for all he can accomplish. I hope I am being crystal clear. Firmly establish your son's understanding that his life has great value and all opportunities are available for him.

Clarity is a useful resource. If it is implemented at the right time, lessons presented in a simple, clear way can open the door to the possibility of greatness. Sister, try to always be crystal clear and on time as you communicate to your son what he needs to know about life. Do your best to keep the lessons age appropriate, so you don't overwhelm him with what should be reserved for another season in his life. Timing is always very important in this process. In Ecclesiastes 3, the Bible says that there is a time for everything. Your ability to discern the perfect time is crucial.

Your son deserves at least the opportunity to chase his dreams. (I didn't say he would catch them.) When he sees another man chasing a dream, why shouldn't he be equally inspired and given the same opportunity to strive to achieve his goals. If he sees another boy scoring a touchdown, he can practice harder and, one day, he may score a touchdown, too. If he enjoys hearing a valedictorian and gets motivated, he can study hard and may achieve the grades it takes to stand in the same spot one day. If he visits a friend's upscale house and is amazed at the amenities, he can work hard in life to achieve financial success. Whatever he sees someone else doing, make sure he knows to not get jealous, envious, or upset. Instead, teach him how to be inspired to reach the same heights.

Let's be crystal clear, no matter what the feat, he can do it. After all, you are raising him to be amazing.

Spiritual Impact

THE STORY OF PETER'S RECOGNITION
OF THE GENTILES' SALVATION

(Acts 11:1–14)

To be recognized for something outstanding is always a special moment for anyone. Perfect Attendance, Most Likely to Succeed, Most Valuable Player, or other types of awards make the recipient's day. Awards turn a frown into a smile. They make the hard work worth it. They give you fuel to keep going. This is why it is so important to recognize the things your son achieves. No matter how great or small, an achievement is still an achievement.

TIME OUT!

The Gentiles are those outside the Hebrew lineage. However, through Jesus' death on the cross and His resurrection, their salvation is also assured. Let me say this right here and now with no reservations, I am so glad I was included in this salvation plan and was given the opportunity for eternal life with my Lord. My sister, if you have accepted Jesus as your Savior and Lord, you were included, too!

And the apostles and brethren that were in Judaea heard that the Gentiles had also received the word of God. And when Peter was come up to Jerusalem, they that were of the circumcision contended with him, saying, Thou wentest in to men uncircumcised, and didst eat with them. But Peter rehearsed the matter from the beginning, and expounded it by order unto them. (Acts 11:1–4)

I can just see how this news was received by the Jewish congregation. The folks who thought they had the good news on lock didn't like having to share it with folks they felt were undeserving.

Sister, make sure you school your son on the fact that there are times when other people don't want you to have what they have, in spite of the fact that you have been granted access.

When Peter was criticized by the Hebrews, he told them the whole story: "I was in the city of Joppa praying, and in a trance I saw a vision" (Acts 11:5). I love how Peter responded. He didn't get upset. He didn't put them in their place. He kept it cool and began to explain, even though he didn't have to.

A certain vessel descend, as it had been a great sheet, let down from heaven by four corners; and it came even to me: Upon the which when I had fastened mine eyes, I considered, and saw fourfooted beasts of the earth, and wild beasts, and creeping things, and fowls of the air. And I heard a voice saying unto me, Arise, Peter; slay and eat. (Acts 11:5–7)

I am amazed as I read Peter's response to his critics. He was crystal clear that the voice of God spoke to him. The plan to include all people in the kingdom of God came from God Himself. Peter could remain totally confident when questioned because he knew he spoke the will of God. Yet when Peter first heard the Lord in his vision, he questioned what he saw. He had doubts and expressed them to God.

You can use this passage of Scripture to teach your son that it is okay when others call on him to explain himself or prove his worth. He can stand firm as Peter did if he knows he stands on a strong foundation—having received guidance and wisdom from God.

When it comes to his goals and dreams, help him learn to hear the inner voice telling him what's right to do. If your son does not know the Lord, it's your responsibility to help him see his need. When he accepts Christ into his heart, the Holy Spirit can dwell therein and assure him that God is with him.

We also read in this passage how Peter responded to the Lord when told to eat foods that were forbidden to the Jewish people: "Not so, Lord: for nothing common or unclean hath at any time entered into my mouth" (Acts: 11:8). (Wow! So I'm not the only one who second guesses what the Lord tells me to do!) Peter had doubts. However, he was not hesitant to express them. And God did not fail to respond to Peter. He not only answered him, but gave him further direction to help him understand more clearly.

From this interaction between Peter and God, you can teach your son to speak up when he feels unsure about something. If what he's being told to do is right, asking questions won't be offensive; it will only provide insight to help him understand what he needs to know.

Your son can also learn a great lesson about obedience through this story about Peter's encounter with God. Even though Peter was uncomfortable with the directions he was given in the vision, he obeyed in faith when God said, "What God hath cleansed, that call not thou common" (Acts 11:9).

Peter's mind could not immediately grasp all God wanted him to learn; so God repeated the message for him.

> And this was done three times: and all were drawn up again into heaven. (Acts 11:10)

Peter gained great knowledge and insight through simple obedience. After Peter heard God's words, he responded with unquestioning submission to God's will, "And, behold, immediately there were three men already come unto the house where I was, sent from Caesarea unto me. And the Spirit bade me go with them, nothing doubting. Moreover these six brethren accompanied me, and we entered into the man's house" (Acts 11:11, 12). We can all learn from Peter's response. Walk in faithful obedience and blessing will follow.

I can only imagine how Peter felt when he found that an angel of God had said, "send men to Joppa, and call for Simon, whose surname is Peter; who shall tell thee words, whereby thou and all thy house shall be saved" (Acts 11:13, 14). Peter must have felt goose bumps when he realized God had spoken to others about him. Peter knew he'd been called to do a great work for God. However, how wonderful it must have been to hear another man speak of his worth. Although we should not serve the Lord in order to receive a reward from men, it is so encouraging to hear others confirm our actions. That's why it's important to tell your son his worth. Let him know why he's special. When he knows you think he's valuable, he will own up to your expectations.

Sister, just as was true with Peter, there will be people who will try to stand in the way of what you and your son should have. But just as he did, press on past those critics; hush them up. This is your son's story. Keep doing what you know is right, and keep helping your son go for his dreams.

The bottom line is this: you and your son deserve the opportunities God brings your way. Some may question you. You may have doubts yourself. However, if you trust and obey the calling the Lord places on your life, you will be victorious. So many good things await you and your son. It might be a tad scary at first to pursue life beyond the norm; but if the Lord is with you, who can be against you? No one! (See Rom. 8:31.) So be like Peter and go for yours.

*M*ama's Story:

THE STORY OF THE NIGHT SHE HELPED ME FIND MY DREAM

Lesson: Your words can clearly motivate.

My mother used a lot of terms or phrases to express her point and to get the message to me about her intentions. Here are a few of my favorites: "Boy, you better not test me." "Son, you do have a brain don't you?" "For the life of me, you're gonna get this if it kills me." Now, my all time favorite was, "Do I make myself clear?" This was the one I remember the most. It's the one that I now use with my own children. She always made sure there was never an issue of clarity regarding anything she taught us or anything she wanted us to understand.

My mother made sure that everyone in the community I grew up in understood how important her children were to her. If we were out past a certain time, she would go looking for us. If there was a problem with a neighbor, she would always take our side until further facts were gathered. If someone messed with us, they quickly realized they were messing with her, also.

My mother never considered the opportunity to accomplish anything as something beyond any one of her children. She always took the position that we were just as good as anyone. I truly believe her belief in me was what motivated me to pursue my own ambitious dreams. The fact that I always heard her tell me I could accomplish any of the things others had accomplished was huge.

Sister, never let your son accept being left out of an opportunity he has a realistic chance of achieving. If it takes effort, encourage him to do whatever it takes. He may think it's too hard; but you can help him devise a plan to break the big steps into manageable pieces. He may feel inferior; but you can be in his ear and cheer him on until he finds his own confidence. He may not be equipped with all he needs for the journey; but you can get him the help he needs. When your son develops a positive dream, when he has discovered what he wants, jump on board with his vision and help him reach his destination.

When I was growing up, I remember I would sit in front of the television day in and day out during football season; I watched every football game I could. It didn't matter if it was college football or professional football; I enjoyed them all. My mother picked up on my passion for football.

You see, sister, one of the things I believe parents have, is the ability to recognize their children's greatest interests. Also, they have the ability to see their children's gifts, and they can have a strong voice in encouraging their children toward successful use of those gifts. You know if he's tech savvy. You know if he's athletic. You know if he's a math whiz. You know. Since you know what his abilities and gifts are, push him toward putting his strengths to use.

My mother saw my interest in football and began to encourage me in that direction. I'll never forget the day she walked into our living room (family room, TV room, or whatever room you want to call it) and caught me locked into a late Monday Night pro football game. She had told me earlier to get to bed, but I had not moved in that direction. Instead of getting on to me for disobeying, she said, "You know that can be you one day don't you?" I couldn't look up at her because my eyes would have shown her that I wasn't sure. She knew I doubted myself, so she kept talking. "Yep, that'll be my boy one day. He'll be running the ball for a touchdown. I see the way you play around here. You have the skills. You can run and you can play. That will be you some day."

Her motivation fueled my desire to play on the grid iron. I had thought about it before she said anything; but

I dared not believe I could until she freed the passion burning deep inside of me. My mom said I could play on the highest level. Honestly, at that point, she probably doubted I *would*; but she told me I *could*. All it took was her belief in me, and I was off to the races with my dream. From that night on, I never looked back.

Even though mom took advantage of the opportunity to speak encouragement into my life, she still got on to me about being disobedient. But she did it in a creative way. This is how it went down: I jumped to my feet and hugged her, saying, "You think I can be in the NFL one day? Really, Mama?" She kissed my jaw and said, "I know you can. But if you don't get the proper rest, you won't do well in school. And if you don't do well in the classroom, no matter how good you play, you can't go to college. If you don't play in college, the scouts can't find you for the NFL. Yep, then all your great talent will go to waste."

I turned off the television so fast you would have thought she paid me a million dollars to do it. In my mind, her words actually connected the dots and showed me why obeying her would get me to my dream. She used psychology to inspire me and make me a better person, student, and football player.

When your son senses he can do something, it is a major step in getting him to accomplish it. Building confidence in him regarding the things he wants to do is key. Confidence comes as a result of first believing that you belong. Sister, if he doesn't feel that he belongs, he will never take that first step; and all journeys begin with that one.

Your ability to be plugged into his every-day routine will be crucial in getting him on the path toward his dreams. Keep an eye on what he really enjoys and pay attention to the things he seems to be very passionate about. Also, help him see the area in which he might be really gifted and push him in that direction. Make sure you play a major role in helping him see that he belongs wherever he is willing to put in the necessary work and dedication. Just because someone else might be more adept at grabbing hold of their dream does not mean that the same opportunity can't come to life for him.

When my mother came to me outside of the locker room after my first game in the NFL, she walked up to me and grabbed my cheeks. She had such pride in her eyes, and we both teared up. She said, "I told you, you could do this. You believed it. You worked hard for it. And now you know you belong here; don't you?" Looking her straight in the eye this time, I said, "Yes, Mama! And I couldn't have gotten here without you."

Athletic Tale

GEORGIA TECH'S GREAT WIN OVER AUBURN

On a beautiful, fall afternoon in downtown Atlanta, the Georgia Tech Yellow Jackets, with freshman Reggie Ball at quarterback, were in dire need of a win. They had lost to Brigham Young University the week before, and spirits were low. Reggie Ball engineered (no pun intended, since Georgia Tech is an engineering school) one of the great wins in Georgia Tech football history—it was a battle against Auburn and a game that would set the pace for Reggie's career.

As the team prepared to meet Auburn, they were inspired by the loss Auburn had suffered at the hands of the University of Southern California. It had been a close game between USC and the team that had been ranked as high as fifth in the country at the start of the season. Georgia Tech fed off the belief that if USC could beat Auburn, so could Tech. This became the rallying cry, plus the fact that there was a long-standing rivalry between Auburn and Georgia Tech.

From the start, Tech made it crystal clear that they could do what USC did—they could win! Tech stopped Auburn on its first possession. On Tech's opening offensive possession, Reggie Ball threw a fifty-five-yard pass deep down the field to wide receiver, Nate Curry. This set up a twenty-two-yard field goal for Dan Burnett. Tech was on the board first. It was clear to everyone watching at home or on television—Tech was serious.

I presently have the honor of being the team chaplain for Tech football. I also had the good fortune of being present at this game. Early on game day, I met with the team and shared a message about belonging on the same field with Auburn. Guess where I got that message from. You guessed it—my mother. I told the team that, if USC could earn a win, so could they. Needless to say, it fired up the team. Georgia Tech went on to defeat Auburn that day and sent a message to the college football world that they *could* do what USC did.

Sister, your son can follow in winning footsteps too. He can go on to accomplish what those ahead of him have already accomplished. He just needs the right motivation and a clear message that he can. This is where you come in.

I often speak on the subject of having a "cheerleader mentality." At all football games, there are cheerleaders whose sole purpose is to cheer on their team and help them on to victory. Well, you are the biggest cheerleader your son will ever have this side of heaven. If you need to, take your pompoms and megaphone and make sure he hears you loud and clear. Cheer him on to the win!

After their win against USC, many Tech players thanked me for telling them they were just as good as powerful USC. They knew it before I told them, but hearing it from someone who cared for them helped them live up to their potential level of play and dominate.

Your son can do big things too. Pump him up; be there with him; help him gain the skills; then sit back and watch him win!

Inspirational Insight
Stephanie's Message

Derrick had me cracking up at the start of this chapter. He knows my pet peeve is drinking out of dirty glasses. See, our three teens take turns washing dishes. They hate that I don't use the paper cups every time I drink something. More times than not, they half wash the glasses. It makes me mad at the rascals just thinking about how they can sometimes be so lazy.

Thankfully, this chapter inspired me. I love drinking sparkling grape juice out of a wine glass because it makes me feel special. It motivates me to keep on keeping on. I toast cheers to myself when I finish a chapter or do something I'm proud of. I have found my own small way to stay upbeat and cheer myself on.

I try to cheer my children on, too. Daily, I strive to paint pictures for them about their future and use every motivational technique I can. I just want them to know they can succeed; they belong; and if they work hard and aren't lazy, their dreams await them. Let me leave you with three things I took away from Chapter Six.

First, *teach him to be motivated*. You just have to get creative with him to keep him going. Always put something out there that will get your son's attention and clear up any doubt about whether or not he can do it. A motivated son can become a successful son. But, motivation can be different for every person. What motivates one person may not motivate another. That's why it is so important for you to pick up on his interest and find ways to get him excited about it.

Secondly, *teach him to identify what he loves*. Kids can't always connect the dots. As a mother who gets to see him in action every single day, you are more than aware of what your son loves to do. You can help him understand his strengths. Sometimes, you can see his passion through the things he watches on television or even in the things he seems to always talk about. Stay attentive to these key areas so you can push him in those directions. Show him that his interest in something could possibly be where his destiny lies.

Finally, *teach him to stay focused on his strengths*. When he's focused, others can't sidetrack him off course.

Derrick is always saying, "If they didn't talk you into it, they can't talk you out of it." Once your son zeros in on what he's good at and what he wants, no one can stop him. When he goes for his dreams, he'll become a better young man because he is a man on a mission.

As moms, we know we can't live our son's life, but we can greatly influence his path. We can hug him when he's sad. We can pray for him when he sleeps. We can tell him he is the best until he starts believing he is the best. Yes, we can make sure we expose him to many wonderful things. If he's intrigued with the Olympics, we can tell him he can be an athlete, too. Even if his dream is far removed from an athletic endeavor, we can help him see the value of training as hard as an Olympian. Whatever area of life he wants to pursue, if he trains with the single-minded devotion of an Olympian, he cannot help but win in life.

These six chapters have moved me to be a better mom. Yes, we moms need motivation too. Everything you do as a mother is designed to drive your son right up next to his opportunity. Just don't let him run out of gas before he gets there. You can't run out of gas either. It's important that you keep yourself going strong. Do what inspires you to keep moving forward. Maybe it's a long hot bath. Maybe it's going to the movies. Maybe it's pouring yourself a nice cold glass of sparkling grape juice and slowly sipping it—like filling yourself up with a treat that says, "Keep on pouring into your son, Mama." You might get tired, frustrated, or angry sometimes, but cheers to you girl! You aren't quitting and you care. Bigger results are on the way. Keep telling yourself and your son that truth. **Keep on raising him, sister!!!**

show him the passion of Paul

Someone once told me, if you have no passion, you have no purpose. If you have no purpose, then what's the point? Now, you can certainly have poorly-guided passion. (We'll explore more about that in a moment.) Hopefully, your passion is fueled by your purpose. Your purpose is what will get you out of bed in the morning. How passionate you are regarding your purpose will determine the kind of fuel (or effort) you put into it—high octane or just plain, old, regularly performing fuel. What I am trying to say, sister, is that not everyone is running on the same stuff. But, when it comes to your son, I am more than confident your passion runs high; he will get nothing less than your A game, which, by the way, is the premium stuff.

It's hard to search the Scriptures and find a more passionate person than Paul. Believe it or not, sister, he was this way before he came to know Christ. He was passionate about what he believed and pursued it with everything he had. You see, his passion before Christ was to hurt Christ; but his passion after meeting Christ, was to help Christ. In both accounts, his passion ran high. However, before Christ his passion was misguided. Paul was fired up but not about the right thing.

Sister, we can get excited or fired up about a lot of things—the car you drive, some of the things talked about at the hair salon, the person who catches your eye . . . you know what I mean. Just make sure what fires you up is the right thing. Things, gossip, and people pale in comparison to getting fired up about the Lord.

Paul thought persecuting Christians was the right thing to do. He pursued them with a passion! He did all he could to make life miserable for them and to cause as much harm to them as he possibly could. Paul thought he was doing the right thing by hurting Christians. He honestly believed it was his purpose in life, and that is why he was so passionate about it. He was wrong.

Believe it or not, there are parents who have a greater passion for other things than they do for their own children. Their passion is misguided; and ultimately, it will not lead toward a positive result for the ones God has entrusted to them. I can't emphasize enough that you must identify your purpose—you are the parent of a young man full of potential. He needs you to be passionately involved in raising him to be all he can be.

Now, you may not believe your son should get all of you. Your son may be competing with something else or someone else in your life. He may not be the purpose that fuels your passion. But, you know what? Any part of you spent on other things leaves less of you to give to him. If that's the case, like Paul, you could be misguided; it may require an eye-blinding experience to get you on the right track. Your passions in life are what really tell the story about you. When you really understand and give first place to your purpose, you can begin to direct your attention toward becoming all you need to become for that purpose to be fulfilled.

TIME OUT!

I almost forgot something important you should know about Paul. He was first named Saul. Why is that significant? I am glad you asked. God brought about a huge change in Saul and changed his name to reflect that Saul had become a new man.

According to what we know about the way in which God works, it is clear that God is in the change business. What does that mean for you? Well God wants to change you into the best version of yourself. He also wants to change your circumstances in ways that will completely blow your mind.

Listen, I know life can be hard. You might have hang-ups about yourself. Possibly, it's hard to stay motivated. You ask yourself how you can inspire your son when you can't inspire yourself. Having the passion to raise your son well is not predominately a matter of your own life; having the passion to parent him well is a matter that involves his life. Why? Because, as his mother, he is your purpose.

Sister, passion can get you through a lot of things you thought you could not get through. It pushes you past the breaking point—that place where you think you are going to lose your mind, or the place where fear of what could happen to him is at an all time high. It is precisely at these moments when passion will fire you up to find a way to see him through. Someone once called this a "want to" attitude. You don't keep going because you have all the answers; and it is in spite of the fact that you have limited help that you don't quit. Your tenacity should rest solely on the mere fact that he is your purpose; that purpose is worth everything you have, and more.

You might ask why Paul possessed so much passion. Paul was passionate, in part, because he was wired that way—it was his personality and nature. But, mostly, Paul was a passionate man because he identified his true purpose. For Paul, his life purpose was the cause of Jesus Christ.

I hope and pray your overriding purpose is for Christ, even more so than raising your son. Nothing means more and nothing will have a more significant impact on your life or your son's. Sister, if you will raise him well, raise him in the truth of the gospel. The secret to raising your son to apprehend his potential starts with your passion. If your passion is first for Jesus and then for your son, look out! Passion is one of the greatest gifts you can ever give him. **Raise him, sister!!!**

a powerful name

Teach
him the
importance
of his name

(Taken from Acts 9:1–13)

 Motivational Point

You and I were born and given a name. We are not responsible for the name we have, but we become responsible for what the name becomes. Our names represent us and tell everyone who we are. Mention a name, and I'm sure you have an impression of what kind of person possesses it. A name doesn't tell the whole story, but it seems to give us an inkling about the person for whom it stands.

What we do with our name and the message we link to it are key as we go about our business of engaging others. We may be doing great damage to our names by the things we do each day. Some lie, steal, kill, and destroy; so their names get dragged through the mud. Or we may be doing great things and building names with which everyone wants to be associated. Some seek truth, are honest, work hard, and are heroes; so their names receive praise. It isn't necessary to do something big in order to receive criticism or praise. However, we have to remember daily that we have a reputation to protect.

It's important to teach your son that whether he does something bad or something good, people are watching. He needs to learn early that it's best to give them something positive to talk about.

You gave your son a name: David, Quashaun, Trey, Octavious; you get the point. I can hear you calling for him. "David, you better get in this house right now!" I can hear you giving him an instruction. "Quashaun, take this five dollars, and go to the store, and get a gallon of milk." I can hear you getting on to him. "Trey, if you want to make it, you can't make Ds on your math test." I can hear you praising him. "Octavious, I'm so proud of you, son." The point is, when you call him, he knows he is important.

Even before the actual birth took place, you went about the business of selecting a name that you thought would be suitable. Finally, you came up with one. Wow, what a proud moment! Then the work began. From birth on, you have had the task of helping your son find his true value. You have tried to instill in your son the power of establishing a good name—one that will be something to be reckoned with. I can imagine you never hoped he'd reach mediocrity or some average success. No! You've always wanted your son's story to be big. You've been grooming him to make his name stand out and be exceptional. You have lived with the hope that, when his name is mentioned, it's immediately associated with something only high achievers experience.

To help him take his name—the one few people yet know—and create a name of success and significance is the goal. Now, this is not an overnight thing. Nor is it an easy thing. However, know it can be done. Your task is to get your son to understand how important he is and what his potential can be. His destiny is much like his social security number; it's his alone—no two people have the same one. Someone may share the same name, but no one shares his identity. Identity, in the grand scheme of things, is associated with what you do. It's tied to who you hang out with. That's why every single thing your son does and every single place he goes defines a bit more of the person your son truly is. This is where the building of that great name begins.

Your son's actions will define him in the eyes of others in a powerful way. If you want him to be seen as a successful student, he needs to be identified as being someone who seems to always be studying. He should always get his homework done. He should prepare for his exams, and his test results should prove his efforts. If you want him to be known as a young man who always pays great respect to his elders, teach him to use, "Yes, sir" and "Yes, ma'am" when responding to adults. And if you want him to be identified as a good and worthwhile person, make sure he understands that friendship can be beneficial or detrimental. Make it clear to him that being picked by the deadbeats and hanging out with them will be detrimental; but if he befriends those who are going somewhere and making something of themselves, the association will be greatly beneficial.

Friendship is not a means of climbing any ladder of success, but the wrong friends can assure your son's path will be much harder, and the association will be detrimental to his goals and dreams. When a new friend comes into your son's life and wants to be his boy, make sure your son understands the importance of choosing his friends wisely. If Jimmy uses drugs and is a trouble maker, help your son understand why they can't be friends. If Calvin is a star athlete and role model, he and your son can be mutually benefited by the friendship. If Larry fights all the time and carries a gun, help your son see all the reasons being friends with Larry could be detrimental to his dreams. If Bobby is holding down a good job and paying his way through school, encourage your son to befriend him. When your son hangs out with guys with negative associations to their name, he is labeled in a bad light. When your son is with folks doing positive things, then, by association, his name has honor. I know it may sound a bit calculating; but when you consider that your son's reputation is at stake, the caution and maneuvering will be worth it. Once you get a poor reputation, it is hard to fix it. This truth can be seen in the life of Saul (who became Paul).

It took the supernatural influence of God Himself through Jesus to fix Saul's rep. He went from persecuting Christians to saving Christians. Once he had an encounter with the living Christ, he was no longer identified as Saul, but he was transformed to Paul—a new identity was formed, a new reputation was shaped, and a new name was established.

So, when folks think of your son's name, I hope good thoughts come. If so, then keep on doing what you're doing because obviously he is on the right track. However, if you know his reputation has been soiled, don't fret. No matter how much your son has messed up, now is the time to help him see the light. You might be frustrated, but pump him up. Tell him he can do it. His name can go from zero to hero. People will say, "Johnzell finally made an A." "I can't believe Chris apologized." "Will said he was sorry." "Zachary stopped bullying people." Your son's name is special. Help him treat it with care.

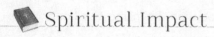 Spiritual Impact

THE STORY OF SAUL EARNING A BAD NAME

(Acts 9:1–13)

What's in a name you might ask? More than you can imagine: attitude, belief, character, disposition, effort, friendship, gratitude, hospitality, independence, justice, kindness, love, mercy, nonviolence, opportunity, promise, quality, respect, sincerity, tolerance, usefulness, victory, wisdom, x-factor, youth, and zero. From A through Z, there is something in every name. Each of these words could easily bring to mind the name of an individual. When you think of a certain person, one of these terms might be fitting.

"And Saul, yet breathing out threatenings and slaughter against the disciples of the Lord, went unto the high priest" (Acts 9:1). This verse makes it clear that none of the words in the list above describe Saul of Tarsus as he was before he met Jesus. Just reading the first couple of verses in the Acts passage can cause severe dislike of this hard, cold man. Saul spoke negative words against God's people and treated them with contempt. Sister, it doesn't take long to identify that Saul had his own way of doing things. If he saw a Christian, he was going to take that person into custody or worse. His actions defined who he was. He was a mean son of a gun. People knew it and he was probably proud of it.

And desired of him letters to Damascus to the syna-
gogues, that if he found any of this way, whether they
were men or women, he might bring them bound unto
Jerusalem. (Acts 9:2)

Saul was truly a man who was motivated by the wrong
things and driven with passion that was misguided.

And as he journeyed, he came near Damascus: and
suddenly there shined round about him a light from
heaven: And he fell to the earth, and heard a voice
saying unto him, Saul, Saul, why persecutest thou me?
And he said, Who art thou, Lord? And the Lord said,
I am Jesus whom thou persecutest: it is hard for thee
to kick against the pricks. And he trembling and aston-
ished said, Lord, what wilt thou have me to do? And
the Lord said unto him, Arise, and go into the city,
and it shall be told thee what thou must do. And the
men which journeyed with him stood speechless, hearing a voice, but seeing no man. And Saul arose from
the earth; and when his eyes were opened, he saw no
man: but they led him by the hand, and brought him
into Damascus, and he was three days without sight,
and neither did eat nor drink. And there was a certain
disciple at Damascus, named Ananias; and to him said
the Lord in a vision, Ananias. And he said, Behold, I am
here, Lord. And the Lord said unto him, Arise, and go
into the street which is called Straight, and enquire in
the house of Judas for one called Saul, of Tarsus: for,
behold, he prayeth. And hath seen in a vision a man
named Ananias coming in, and putting his hand on him,

that he might receive his sight. Then Ananias answered,
Lord, I have heard by many of this man, how much evil
he hath done to thy saints at Jerusalem. (Acts 9:3–13)

Saul had what we call a "moment"; but not just any
moment. It was a powerful moment that not only restored
Saul's name, it changed his name. The very One Saul fought
against, asked him to fight on the side of the Son of God.
Shoot; I'd need a moment, too, if I were Saul. This enemy of
Christ had his reputation and his identity re-established and
renewed through an eye-opening, blinding experience—as
he traveled along the road, Saul met the resurrected Jesus.
Afterward, Saul was blinded and taken to a city where a
man named Ananias had received a word from God telling him to pray for Saul's sight to be restored. Saul's reputation and name was so infamous as a result of what he
had done that Ananias didn't want to help; but he obeyed
God and Saul was healed. No matter how he felt about
Saul, God told Ananias to help anyway. As a result, Saul
was converted.

After this experience, Saul no longer persecuted Christians. He began a process of showing people he had
changed. So by Acts 13 everyone knew that he was a new
man—Paul. He preached Jesus to the unsaved and taught
Christians about their new life in Christ. He changed completely and for the better. His name became synonymous
with life instead of death. This ex-persecutor of Christians

ended up writing most of the books of the New Testament and is noted to be the most powerful evangelist of his day.

Just as Saul was, we can be set in our ways and blind to the truth. But when God shows up, He can change things. He can make us think. He can make us take a look at ourselves. He can take all the worst aspects of the person we have been, change us from the inside out, and give us a new name and a new life. Sometimes, our actions toward others have caused them to turn from us and refuse us help. Thankfully, God gives grace. No matter how badly we've lived our lives in the past, if we will allow Him to open our blind eyes and see the salvation He has provided through His Son, Jesus, we can be changed as quickly and as surely as Saul. And our lives can then be used to impact our world, just as Paul impacted the early church.

Sister, it all comes down to what your son does with his name. It's not the name that's been given at birth that can become legendary; instead, it's the name he gains in life that can become legendary through the things he does with it. Help your son see that, like Paul, the Lord has a plan for his life and will give him the vision to see the truth that is before him.

Mama's Story:

THE STORY OF JUST A LITTLE DAB WILL DO

Lesson: Your name makes a difference.

I was kind of famous in my home and very popular in the community. This was not due to the name I was given at birth, but because of a nickname. They called me Dab. (That's right. Don't laugh. I bet your son will have his fair share of nicknames, also. He may be called: Skeeta, Pokie, Short bread; you get the point.) It's funny. My mother came up with the name because I had a habit of hanging around the kitchen. At a very young age, I found myself always wanting to taste my mother's cooking before it was ready. She would respond with the statement, "You want a little dab, don't you." Before I knew it, the nickname had stuck.

As you well know, it doesn't take long for the word to get out. First, my brother and sister started using the nickname. Then the neighbors referred to me as Dab. I can tell you for a fact, after the day she came up with Dab, my mother never called me Derrick again. Make no mistake, she knew my name. However, there was a reputation she established by giving me this nickname.

I remember being upset that folks weren't calling me Derrick. Mom sat me down and explained why I should be really proud of the meaning behind "Dab." She said that the only thing any situation needed to make it better was a little "dab." "A little Dab will do ya" was her motto for me. During that talk, I came to understand the expectation behind her name for me. She knew the world would know me by my birth name, but I was her Dab, and her expectations of me would not change.

Honestly, she was so right about my disposition. I could light up a room when I walked into it. I had a very encouraging personality that seemed to give everyone the idea that life was okay. My reputation as "Dab" followed me into every endeavor I entered. Though my college schoolmates would know me as Derrick, it was still Dab they were experiencing. I remember Mom would say, "If you put a little dab in the friendship, they will love you as I do."

When I was finally drafted by the Atlanta Falcons of the NFL, I remember my mom saying to me that all the Falcons needed was a little dab to make the difference. I guess her impression of me was that I would go through life taking great confidence in the fact that I would have a positive impact in my associations and change things for the better. I would like to think she was right. If I surveyed the people I have met over the many years: college friends, professional football peers, my ministry partners, and even my own family, I would like to believe they all would say that a little dab blessed them.

Such can be the same with your son. There is something great about what his name can say to the world. You have to help him understand what that worth is. It's too important to take lightly and too meaningful for you to ignore. He can be a difference maker. His name says so.

Athletic Tale

THE TAMPA BAY DEVIL RAYS' CHANGE THEIR NAME

There are clear and necessary reasons when a name change would be fitting. Usually, there is something that has made you image conscience. Let's face it, image to most of us means everything. We, as a nation, spend billions on health and wellness efforts to either change how we look or improve our health. All this time and attention is given to our physical image; we consider it highly important and worth the effort to change.

But there is also the image that results from the things we've done and the perception others have about us. If this image is going to change, then there are but two things you can do about it. One is to change the way you do things. The other is to do something similar to what Paul did. This was the case for the Tampa Bay Devil Rays.

Before the 2008 season, the Devil Rays decided to drop the word "devil" from their name and be called simply the

Tampa Bay Rays. Talk about an immediate impact! The Devil Rays had always been the joke of the American league. They had very poor fan support, no real impact players, and they were making no one in the Tampa area very happy. (I am going to go ahead and state my opinion. Dropping the word "devil" from anything is a win in my book.)

Sister, there is something to be said for being image conscience. No one wants a reputation for being a loser. Neither did Tampa Bay. They no longer wanted to be associated with the poor image they suffered under. So, they decided they would do something about it. The Devil Rays became the Tampa Bay Rays.

Changing their name and ultimately their image changed the way the team played. Players stepped up. Coaches worked harder. Fans showed up. They were the Rays and they were going in a new, winning direction. Everyone who was a part of the organization bought into this mindset. You won't believe this, but once the Devil Rays changed their name to the Rays they went on to win the American league pennant that very season.

TIME OUT!

The pennant is the league championship in baseball.

What the Rays were able to accomplish after their name was changed is just an amazing thing. I don't believe it was a matter of coincidence. It was a matter of image. They no longer had the old, loser reputation stuck in their heads. With the change of name came a change of attitude. If you ask me, the attitude of the entire organization turned.

Sister, if your son's self-image is not the best, a change could be just what he needs. You may not wish to change his name; but together, you and your son can change what he and others think of his name. Like the Rays, with a new attitude and a renewed view of himself, your son can win in life, too.

Inspirational Insight
Stephanie's Message

I have to admit I'm emotional reading this chapter. I'm not sure if you know this or not, but our son was adopted. The Lord allowed Derrick and me to become parents to Leon Thomas when he was ten years old. Our son suffered severe loss early in his life. He lost his mother and older brother when he was in the third grade. Real hard stuff. But God brings hope in darkness.

Leon so wanted to be a part of our family. I truly wanted him to belong. So in addition to becoming his parents, we went before the judge to request a legal name change. Leon Thomas became Dustyn Leon Moore. He was so proud, and Derrick and I were so happy.

Here is what I have come to understand over the many years of my own life. Change is sometimes not a choice. As thrilled as I was that God brought Dustyn to our family, it still breaks my heart that he lost his mother; that could never be changed. However, when life happens, circumstances suggest that the best way to survive is to make positive changes wherever you can. I want to leave you with three reasons why change of mind, attitude, and name is a welcomed idea to teach your son.

First, *teach him that his name should be positively known*. Your son should understand that people will build a perception of him through the things he does. He will be called out for the good and bad. Explain to him that he is daily building up his name or tearing it down by his actions. If his name has a negative association, tell him it's time for a change.

Secondly, *teach him the importance of his name*. You named your son. You have expectations of what his name should stand for. Make sure he knows that. Help him see what you see in him. Lift him up so he can know his worth.

Lastly, *teach him his name will take him places*. Help your son understand that, when people think positively of him, more opportunities will come his way. Make sure he knows that his name could also lead him into trouble if he doesn't fix any negative perceptions others may have of him. If your son wants to go somewhere great, then he needs to take special care of his name. He also needs to stay aligned with others who take good care of their names.

I know without having to ask you that all you want for your son is for him to have a chance to succeed in this life. You want to see him on top. You want to help him get there. You thought carefully when you gave him his name so he could do something with it. You love him.

When our son needed a new name, I gave him three choices for a first name. It had to start with a "D" because Derrick's name starts with a "D." It had to have an "S" in it because my name starts with an "S." So the choices were Dallas, Dawson, or Dustyn. You know his choice: Dustyn. Derrick loved the choice. He told Dustyn he had received a new life, and it was time to "dust" himself off and walk with pride. We kept Leon as his middle name because it connects him with his biological mom. And he was happy to become a Moore because he would have the last name of a family who loved him unconditionally. My son's name is special, just as your son's name is special. Let's help our boys live up to their worth. **Raise him, sister!!!**

his-story lesson

Teach him

to learn

from

the past.

(Taken from Acts 13:16–30)

 Motivational Point

My wife and I love a good story. Stephanie is a fiction writer. Her goal is to write novels that teach lessons. But, I love watching the news. I learn what not to do from seeing what knuckle-heads have done to get themselves in trouble. Now that Stephanie and I are older, we are both history buffs and enjoy the true stories of the past. We often find ourselves channel surfing and land on the Discovery channel. It's amazing to learn what people have done before us; we can analyze the road they've traveled and see how best to find our way based on historical people and the journeys they faced.

Of course, there is no greater history lesson than the story of Jesus Christ coming to save a lost world. His-story is a model of perfection and a lesson on forgiveness with a dose of benevolence. It is the greatest story ever told. And there are lessons from the life of Christ that serve as the information center for our own future success.

Sister, there are some major lessons that your son needs to learn if he is to get to where you would like to see him someday. The things at which we see others succeed or fail can provide us with valuable information that will aid us as we step into the future. To step forward blindly is risky. It's always best to know where the next step leads before you take it.

In the Bible, we read about Jesus meeting many people and teaching many lessons. Each of His messages contains truth that is applicable in our pursuit of excellence.

In John 8:2–11, we read a powerful story that teaches us about forgiveness. In Matthew 26:36–45, we read an account from Jesus' life that teaches the importance of prayer and watchfulness. And in John 2:13–17, we gain a great deal of insight about honesty, integrity, and holiness from Jesus' reaction to the money changers in the temple. Take the time to revisit these tremendous stories and pull from them the lessons that are still so important, even in our day and time.

Lessons from the past can be either positive or negative; but they all do one thing your son needs in order to walk forward with confidence: they will teach him that the past is a gateway to the future. Someone once said, "The past is to be remembered because it might need repeating; or repeating the past may not be the thing to do." Making the distinction between past actions to avoid and ones to repeat can be as simple as seeing the results of the choices of those who walked before us.

Check out this story. Antonio just wanted a quick way to make some loot. The solution seemed simple—he went to rob the corner store. Well, things got out of hand and he ended up shooting some customers. When the cops came, they shot Antonio. Days later, a grieving mother buried her son. All this, just because he wanted to make a quick buck. When it comes to your son, this is a story you don't want to become his-story.

In contrast, William wanted a better life. He worked two jobs until he saved up enough money to go to technical school. While in school to be an auto mechanic, he got a job at a mechanic's shop. Once he had his degree, he had gained favor with the owner. When the owner opened another shop, William became the manager. He gained money and self-worth. When it comes to your son, this is a story worthy of becoming his-story.

You see, sister, we live in a results-driven society. We want to know the expected results of any and all situations. The neat thing about the past is that it allows us to see the results of situations and circumstances that took place before us.

TIME OUT!

Grandfather Perry prefaced most statements by saying, "I mean, in other words . . ." I always found the way he clarified his point of view to be remarkable. It is always a good idea to make sure your son clearly understands your words to him.

My wife's grandfather, Rev. Dewey Perry, was 91 years old when he went on to be with the Lord. In his wisdom, Reverend Perry explained that the past gives us the answers in advance of our current situation. He'd say, "If you want to go somewhere, be with someone who is going somewhere. If they ain't about nothing, don't hang with 'em." I preach his wise advice to my own son, today.

Most situations, if not all, that will take place with you and your son, mirror situations others have experienced in the past. Talk about knowing the future results of a situation! Well, all you have to do is research your situation and discover the actions and reactions of those who faced the same circumstance in the past. You will be amazed at the wisdom and the accuracy of the insight you will gain into your present-day situation. Following the lessons learned by the ones who have been in the same position can assure you a favorable outcome. Teaching your son that history is a valuable asset to him will provide a major component in his development. Who knows, it could even give him a greater appreciation for his history course at school.

Your son's story has a greater chance of unfolding well when he fully understands the value of the past and the answers it holds for his future. This is where you come in, sister. You have to take the time to cover with him the things and situations of the past that render certain results. The lessons you focus on from the past need to be both positive and negative. These valuable lessons are "difference makers" for him as he approaches the most critical events in his life. Giving your son a reference point will be a huge advantage to him. If he is equipped with the ability to glean wisdom from the choices of others in those life-changing moments, look out! He will be equipped with the information he needs to avoid destructive actions and be enabled to capitalize on opportune moments.

Sister, I'll let you in on a little secret: if you want your son to go forward successfully, all you have to do is look back, find positive examples, and share the stories that can lead him to his destination as surely as a road map. If you want him to avoid major destructive moments (and I know you do), all you have to do is point toward examples of poor choices made by others in the past and share the harsh outcomes. He'll get the message and avoid the same mistakes.

Your son needs to know where he comes from. He needs to know the sacrifices made on his behalf by those who have gone before him. He should understand what happens to men when they cut corners and do wrong and, conversely, what great things lie ahead for men who do things right. Tell him the hard facts. If he sees your passion for history, he will embrace the past and become better because of it.

 Spiritual Impact

THE STORY OF PAUL'S ACCOUNT
OF THE THE HISTORY OF A PEOPLE

(Acts 13:16–30)

I have to confess, when I was in school, I was not necessarily into history. That doesn't mean I didn't see the value it presents. You might not be a history buff, but knowing the past has value for your son. So, let's take a look at Paul's account of the history of Israel:

> Then Paul stood up, and beckoning with his hand said, Men of Israel, and ye that fear God, give audience. The God of this people of Israel chose our fathers, and exalted the people when they dwelt as strangers in the land of Egypt, and with an high arm brought he them out of it. (Acts 13:16, 17)

Sister, any time you give your son a lesson on his history, it will open a door to his future. You see, the two are not disconnected. They run side-by-side, though they take place in two different times. If you don't know where you've been, it's going to be hard to really appreciate where you're going. Even more so, when you know where other people have been and how they got there, you can better know how to get to where you are trying to go. Take note of God's work in the lives of the Hebrews:

> And about the time of forty years suffered he their manners in the wilderness. And when he had destroyed seven nations in the land of Chanaan, he divided their land to them by lot. (Acts 13:18, 19)

When God wants to move you into your future, He sometimes takes His time doing it. It has always been true that we don't necessarily arrive at our destination when we want to, but when God thinks we are ready. It was 450 years before God gave the Israelites the prophet Samuel (Acts 13:20).

> And after that he gave unto them judges about the space of four hundred and fifty years, until Samuel the prophet. (Acts 13:20)

Every detail of the past holds very important information that will unlock your son's future. Knowledge is power; and when you have power, you can empower others. Just make sure it's power under control. God removed King Saul, Saul/Paul's namesake, from power because of his lack of faith and control (Acts 13:21-23).

> And afterward they desired a king: and God gave unto them Saul the son of Cis, a man of the tribe of Benjamin, by the space of forty years. And when he had removed him, he raised up unto them David to be their king; to whom also he gave testimony, and said, I have found David the son of Jesse, a man after mine own heart, which shall fulfil all my will. Of this man's seed hath God according to his promise raised unto Israel a Savior, Jesus. (Acts 13:21–23)

Now, here is an important piece of history! Jesus' direct blood line traces back to David. This is what I call total inclusion.

> When John had first preached before his coming the baptism of repentance to all the people of Israel. And as John fulfilled his course, he said, Whom think ye that I am? I am not he. But, behold, there cometh one after me, whose shoes of his feet I am not worthy to loose. Men and brethren, children of the stock of Abraham, and whosoever among you feareth God, to you is the word of this salvation sent. (Acts 13:24–26)

Know this, to know who God is and be in awe of Him is the first major history lesson your son really needs to know.

Teach him to always fear God. Not a scared fear, but a reverential fear.

Sister, be like Paul. Be confident as you remind your son of the great salvation God provided through Jesus Christ:

> For they that dwell at Jerusalem, and their rulers, because they knew him not, nor yet the voices of the prophets which are read every sabbath day, they have fulfilled them in condemning him. And though they found no cause of death in him, yet desired they Pilate that he should be slain. And when they had fulfilled all that was written of him, they took him down from the tree, and laid him in a sepulcher. But God raised him from the dead. (Acts 13:27–30)

It's important to understand that your past can be raised, as well. Not raised up so as to come up against you; but raised up to help you.

Most of us want nothing to do with our past. We spend our lives running from it—things we've done that we are not so proud of, people we've hurt who we really should have helped. Don't let the past be an enemy! Instead, let it be a resource that opens the gateway to the future.

$\mathcal{M}$ama's Story:

MY MOTHER'S STORY ABOUT MY GRANDDAD.

Lesson: Modeling greatness makes you
greater.

If I were to just state facts, most people would consider
that my mom's history contained little to celebrate or
emulate. She had less than a high school education. Most
of her life, she lived below the line of economic empow-
erment. She was a single mom raising three children and
every day was hard. However, she always had a positive
outlook. Though her circumstances were sometimes difficult, nothing kept her down. Oh no, sister! My mother
was strengthened by leaning on her history.

You see, my mother's father, Mr. Luscious Bruce,
always held a smile. He never said a negative word about
anything or anyone. He loved life tremendously. His legacy was a clear message to live life to the fullest and
make the best of whatever life brings. His positive way
of facing life rubbed off on my mother.

I remember, one cold winter night, we came home
and couldn't wait to watch an episode of *Sanford and Son*.
All of us enjoyed laughing at Redd Foxx. We got to the
door and the porch light was off. My mom thought that
was odd. My older brother got us inside and flicked the

light switch. Nothing happened. My sister brushed by me to turn on the television, but it, too, failed to power up. You should have seen the four of us trying to turn on everything that had a switch, all to no avail. My mom went back to the front door and saw a note from the electric company notifying her that our power was cut off. My siblings and I were panicking. No lights, no television, no power! This was horrible! We whined while my mother worked. She found the candles she had tucked away. She grabbed the flashlight. She also got the blankets. Since we couldn't see, she took us, one at a time, to our rooms to get our night clothes.

When my mom and I were alone, I saw a tear fall from her eyes. I said, "Mom, it's okay. You'll get the lights on tomorrow." She held me and said, "I sure will, son; but I'm not crying because I'm sad, I'm crying because I'm happy." At this point, I was confused. We were going to be cold with no heat; we couldn't see, and our food might spoil because of no electricity; yet, she was happy. Huh? As I got into my pajamas she said, "This reminds me of a time when I was a little girl. A similar thing happened. But it was one of the best nights of my childhood. You see, Dab, my dad turned our dark night into a time of fun. And just like we did back then, tonight we're going to have a slumber party. No, we won't watch the television, but we'll tell stories; and our time together will be

special. My dad taught me that there is good in every situation. Even in the dark, I see light.

We went on to have a blast that night. We told stories. (Mine was the best, of course.) We also told our
mom things that were important in our lives. The sharing time was priceless. My mom also used our "slumber
party" as a great teaching moment. She explained to us
that you must pay bills in order to keep the lights on. We
had a tough month, but a great night.

The stories she would tell of her father's incredible
devotion to his family were nothing short of hard to
believe. She said he was the hardest working man she
had ever known. Working was something that was just
in his blood. She said he was the most loving father any
daughter could ever have had. She said he would wake
early in the morning and make sure his family had a
meal to eat. He would seldom allow his wife to cook
breakfast, and most mornings he would bring her
breakfast in bed. (I inherited that trait, as I like getting up early each morning and preparing meals for my
own family.)

I vaguely remember my grandfather. I was told he
would often walk around the community holding me;
though I was too young to remember him doing this. My
mother told me I was the apple of his eye. She also said I
was just as crazy about him and never wanted to let go

of his neck. I felt so connected to this great man, and I just needed her to tell me more.

My mother took a chapter from my grandfather's life to raise me and my two siblings. She spoke often of her own deep devotion to her family and maintained a great respect for what her father was able to do. The most amazing fact about my grandfather was how much he did with very little money. Mom called him a survivor. He was not only her father but was the handyman when things needed fixing. He was a tutor when they needed help with homework. Mom told us that, for someone with limited academic skills, her father sure did help them find answers to their questions. Sister, this is called commitment to someone you love.

My mother said she and her family never felt like they were missing anything. I guess she felt that her father was everything to them, and it showed. He was the standard for devotion in their house, and my mother learned the value of committed love. She passed this value on to her children, as well.

Teach your son about people who have done extraordinary things. Their stories will inspire him and equip him with what it takes to go forward with optimism in his own life. His role models need not be family members; a role model can be anyone who has left a positive message through their life choices. For example, tear a page from the life of Thurgood Marshall, a Supreme

Court Justice. Use his life to teach your son about integrity, fairness, and honor. Share with your son about the life of Langston Hughes, poet, writer, and playwright. Make sure your son knows the power of creativity, self-expression, and literature. Tell him about Hank Aaron, an African American baseball player who soared through the Negro leagues all the way to the major leagues; he became an icon because of his hard work, perseverance, and determination.

There are examples all around; but you, my sister, are the one example who carries the greatest level of influence. You, your choices, and your life are becoming the history that your son will someday draw from; maybe even talk or write about.

That night in the dark opened my eyes. My mom could have felt worthless because our lights were turned off. Instead, she took responsibility and made sure we were stronger, wiser, and better because of the incident. That's powerful, isn't it?

There is no one who touches your son's life in the way you do. The way you raise him in spite of adversity is his-story that will inspire his future.

If you can't buy your son that new outfit, make sure the clothes he has are cleaned and tell him he looks good. He'll smile. If you can't take him out to eat, make sure you teach him how to cook and tell him homemade meals come from the heart. He'll be glad he's full. And if you ever find yourself with no power, make sure he knows the One who holds all the power. You turn to God when darkness falls, and He will see you through.

Hold your head up, my sister. If you make the most out of life, like my granddad did, you will be teaching your son to stay upbeat, also. He's modeling your behavior. Give him something great to model.

Athletic Tale

TRACK STAR LOPEZ LOMONG'S DREAM TO BECOME AN OLYMPIAN

The story of Lopez Lomong is one that reaches deep into the very core of what it means to be inspired by a past event. His actions in the face of brutality and cruelty were nothing short of amazing.

Lopez was one of the so-called "lost boys" of the Sudan Civil War. At age six, he was a refugee among thousands of boys confronted by rebel soldiers. He was forcibly "recruited" for war and trained to carry an AK-47 gun. Risking his young life to gain freedom, Lopez crawled his way out of the rebel camp and ran all the way to Kenya.

TIME OUT!

Sister, when you want it badly enough, nothing will prevent you from finding a way of escape.

As it turned out, his flight from rebel captivity would be Lopez's first experience in running; but it would not be his last. For ten years, he lived in a refugee camp in Kenya. Running became a way to escape his hunger.

One particular night, he spent five shillings to watch the Olympics on a camp television. He got a glimpse of one of the greatest Olympians of all time, the blazing-fast Michael Johnson. Michael was a world class sprinter and gold medal winner in multiple events. In the words of Lopez:

> I saw Michael Johnson running the 400 meter final and he ran incredibly fast. What really inspired me so much is that when he went to receive the medal, I saw the tears come out of his face. In Africa, a grown-up person cannot cry like that. I thought, Why did he cry? He just won the race, he wasn't last. But, eventually, I ended up seeing that he was running behind something bigger than himself—he was running for his country. From that moment, I said I would like to run for that country one day; and he became my role model from that point.

After ten long years in the refugee camp, a Catholic, charitable organization brought Lopez to America. He competed in high school and college level track, and became a naturalized citizen of the U.S. in 2007. The stage was set for Lopez's dreams to become reality.

Lopez had such deep history to draw on. His past as a captive child who ran to escape the brutality of rebel soldiers fueled him. His experience of running to escape his hunger prepared him. His desire to run for a country because he was so moved by the emotions of Michael Johnson was a difference-maker in his life. His past experiences motivated him to run toward his own goal.

Lopez's reliance on his past was the very thing that continued to serve as the catalyst for his success, even in the London Olympics. The single night he spent in front of the television watching Michael Johnson run the 400 meters and win gold changed Lopez's world. He went on to compete as a U.S. Olympian in the 2008 and 2012 Olympic Games.

Sister, I am amazed that there are both positive and negative experiences from our past that have the ability to inspire us in the present. Embracing this element of our lives is crucial; it can be used to push us to the next level of opportunity.

Your son needs his past to inspire him today and all his tomorrows. Reaching back to that past is key to reaching goals and touching dreams. The most incredible reality is that his present moment will someday serve as his past experience. His past experience will help him overcome his present day challenges.

As a child, Lopez was overcome by the magnitude of Michael Johnson's tears after receiving that gold medal. He mentally seized that moment and used it to propel him to the very place Michael Johnson had reached—he became a U.S. Olympian runner.

It's been said that we ought to forget the past. There is some truth to that statement, and the pain of some things is best forgotten. But even those painful things can help us to be better today. We need to leave the pain behind but take the lessons we learn with us into tomorrow. All the experiences we have faced can be lessons to glean from to really thrive in the present.

Lopez ran his way to the Olympic Games all because of circumstances from his past that inspired him. Sister, make sure you are able to point to something from your son's past that he can use in his present. You have to help him learn how to analyze moments, so he can take a lesson from whatever situations he faces. If you do, his tomorrow will be gold medal worthy.

Inspirational Insight

Stephanie's Message

This chapter touched my heart. Derrick mentioned my granddad, Reverend Dewey E. Perry, Sr., and it just reminds me how much I miss him and my two grandmothers. My dad's mom, Lizzie Mae Perry, was a spunky something. She didn't take any stuff and she taught me how to be a strong woman and go after my dreams. My mother's mom, Viola Roundtree, was more laidback. She was mild and sweet and taught me how to be gracious and serve others. I so miss them, but their legacy lives on in me.

I was fortunate both my grandmothers got to meet my children before they went on to be with God. Seeing them look at my kids with love and watching them pray over them was moving. I now tell my kids that their great-grandparents' prayers are carrying them. Here are some points that I hope can carry your son.

First, *teach him history can help when it comes to his maturity*. Obviously, the greatest challenge for young people is that their youth can sometimes get in the way of their growth. When they grow, they move from a place of immaturity to a place of maturity. As your son grows (not only physically but in the areas of understanding), he will began to get the message that his past provides him with valuable experiences he can lean on as he moves along the road of life. Sister, make sure you are always training his thoughts to glean from what's behind him to help him go forward. Tell him what others have done, and help him analyze how he can grow better from the knowledge.

Secondly, *teach him history can help when it comes to his achievements*. Girl, we all need as much help as we can get in trying to accomplish the things in life that satisfy us and give us a feeling of success. Point your son to people of the past who will inspire him. Use these people and their stories to motivate him as much as you can. If you have identified where his interests really lie, point him in the direction of the people who have found success in that area. Convince him that, if they can do it, he can, as well. Lopez did!

Lastly, *teach him history can help when it comes to his beliefs*. If he can ever get to the point where he has completely bought in to the concept that the past is a gateway to the future, lookout, girl! There is something back there that can help him. Don't let him lose sight of the fact that there are positives he can draw from the past that can be difference makers in his life. When he really believes it, he will begin to take into account what the past can teach him about his current moment and all his tomorrow moments. The past is a classroom of information that you can use to equip him as he grows into the man that you want him to be.

Yeah, I miss my grandparents. I'm sure there are loved ones you miss dearly, as well. You probably know the old hymn, *When We All Get To Heaven*. Well, though I don't know what it will be like, I do believe the song and know "what a day of rejoicing that will be!" Until then, let's remember those who have gone before us. We should reflect on their mistakes, and try not to relive them. We should smile thinking about their achievements and hope to recreate them. We should take comfort in the times they prayed for us and strive to live up to their expectations.

There may even be people we haven't met who inspire us. For me, it's talented author, Alex Haley. (I think God's given me a Roots type book that I'm supposed to write someday.) Mr. Haley took us to a place in time that most of us couldn't imagine. The story of slavery he revealed, though trying, was powerful. That story and this chapter teach us that there is a wealth of information in history that can help us now.

Make sure your son knows as much about his past as he can, so he can do great things as he writes his-story. You're not parenting him alone. **You've got the past to help raise him, sister!!!**

mistaken identity

Teach him to not get things twisted.

(Taken from Acts 14)

✦ Motivational Point

Sister, you know what is said about African American men, don't you? Yeah, that's right. It is said that we are a whole lot alike. No, I'm not talking about physical features: height, weight, skin tone, or complexion. No, ma'am! I am talking about situations, circumstances, and conditions through which we can easily be stereotyped. Comments are made often: He's lazy. He's no good. He's a trouble maker. He's a bum. He ain't never gon' be nothing. He's a deadbeat. And many other comments far worse. Keep smiling! In some ways, we might deserve it.

While I admit some of us have let the women in our lives down, to lump all black men into this category is unfair. To say that all black men aren't worth anything is just plain not true. I'm sure you know some black men who don't fit this mold. Am I right?

Yes, there are a great percentage of African American men who are incarcerated; but there are more of us who aren't. You see, sister, just because we are all of the same ethnicity doesn't mean we have the same behavior tendencies. We are all fundamentally responsible for the choices we make and must live with the outcome of those choices.

Don't get it twisted. For every young brother I know who allowed situations, circumstances, and conditions to deny him his freedoms and opportunities to succeed, I know three other brothers who took control of their lives and used negative aspects of life as stepping stones to take advantage of opportunities. Of the four brothers I mention, one turned to crime; but the three others went to college. One went to killing; the three others went to work. One got high on crack; the three others got high off the Word of God. Choices were made by all four individuals. But not all choices made were bad ones.

Teach your son how to take full advantage of every opportunity. He needs your help to resist allowing negative circumstances to cause him to get it twisted and take the easy way. Most times, the easy way leads to trouble. Help your son understand that hard work pays off.

I am so saddened when I hear of young men with the world at their feet, young men who just happen to be African American, getting caught up in the wrong set of circumstances and finding themselves between a rock and a hard place. As we adults know getting caught in a tough situation because of our bad choices is rough stuff. I do understand that a young man could find himself in a bad place because of some unfair circumstances; but in a lot of situations, our young men find themselves in trouble because they placed themselves there through their own poor choices. By trying to take the easy way, young men can end up in a place they can't easily escape. Trouble is easy to get into, but very difficult to get out of.

Make sure you communicate to your son that he must avoid self-inflicted wounds. Drugs and alcohol can ruin his mind. Hanging with the wrong crowd—the ones doing nothing and headed nowhere—can ruin his future. Going to school only to clown around and hang out can ruin his education. He needs to know that you're keeping it real with him. He needs to know you are on his side. He needs to realize you are not getting on him to keep him down, but with the hope he will grab hold of your message and use it to help himself rise up. Honestly, it will take everything in him to avoid outside troubles, let alone those that come from inside the camp. Sister, behavior patterns start to take shape early. You should start the process of teaching him to avoid the pitfalls of "the easy way" from the ground up. This is why your influence at the early stages of his development is so vital.

It's important that you understand your son is watching you. If you want him to be responsible, you must be responsible. If you want him to work hard, he must see you working hard. If you want him to make wise choices, you must make wise choices. We all need a "gut check" from time to time—an objective, honest look at our behaviors and attitudes. Consider this yours.

What can you do to take your game up another level so your son will do the same? Maybe you need to go back to school to further your own education. Maybe you need to apply for a better job. Maybe you need to spend more quality time with your son. I don't know what your "maybe" is; but you do, so get to it!

The identity you want for your son can become reality; but make no mistake, your own worth and value is his role model and godly example. He needs to see you in God's Word, on your knees, and living right. Our true identity is in Christ. However, we must stay connected with the Lord to fully exercise all that's in us.

You remember my Special Teams coach don't you? Frank Ganze was his name. I spoke of his famous quotes earlier in the book. Here's another: "We are what we repeatedly do; therefore, excellence is not an act. Instead, it's a habit." If excellence is something you want for your son, don't allow his identity to be diluted by someone else's. Make sure he understands that his identity is incredibly important and must be protected at all times. To use the vernacular, you and God didn't make no junk. Your son needs to be the person God created him to be, and you need to allow him to become that person. However, you cannot allow your son's actions to degenerate into behaviors that result in him being thrown in a cell and locked away. No matter how many times he may tell you his negative behavior is just an expression of his identity, you and God know better.

Everybody needs to know what your son is about. Teach him to be about getting things done that will move him in the direction of his dreams. Help him see his daily choices are either moving him toward his goals or away from them.

I am told that identity theft in our world is a big deal. If someone gets hold of your social security number, your driver's license, or any important, private information, they will have enough to tap into your world and tamper with your identity. You must take great care and go the extra mile to keep your identity secure and do everything you can to protect yourself.

In the same way, you must help your son protect his identity. Help your son establish who he is so that there is no mistaking him or his behavior for that of someone else. If his identity is firmly established and protected, when a student's iPad gets stolen, all the students will know your son was not the thief. When someone cheats on a test, the teacher will know your son was not involved. When a fib is told at school, the principal will know your son was not a part because he will see your son as a truthful young man. When bad behavior shows up, everyone will know your boy is innocent because of his reputation for being honest and full of integrity. His character will back him up.

Sister, you have to have a passion to get your son to understand the importance of his reputation. You can't consider it a bother or an interruption to your flow of life. Instead, you have a chance to invest in your son in such a way that your return will far exceed your investment. Now, I don't know about you, but I love it when that happens. It's always good when you get more out than you put in. In the world of economics, that's called profit. In your world with your son, that's called love. Don't get it twisted in this stage of his life; no one loves him more than you.

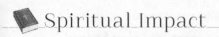# Spiritual Impact

THE STORY OF PAUL AND BARNABAS BEING CONFUSED FOR GODS

(Acts 14:8–15)

We can relate to what happened to Paul and Barnabas. No one really likes to be confused for someone else. It's even worse when your identity is smudged by a negative association. To be wrongly accused of anything is a bad deal.

In the case of Paul and Barnabas, the people of Lystra wrongly identified the men as gods. I can tell you this, sister, anytime there is a little-g god involved, it can never be mistaken for the true and only big-G God. Those folks had these boys wrongly identified.

> And there sat a certain man at Lystra, impotent in his feet, being a cripple from his mother's womb, who never had walked. (Acts 14:8)

There was a man there whose identity was wrapped up in his physical impairment. He had been lame since birth. I'm sure folks took pity on him.

> The same heard Paul speak: who stedfastly beholding him, and perceiving that he had faith to be healed. (Acts 14:9)

Paul took notice of this man. What a great parallel between what Paul saw in the lame man and what you see in your son. Paul saw faith and you see potential. Paul told that man to stand, and he did more than that; he lept!

> Said with a loud voice, Stand upright on thy feet. And he leaped and walked. (Acts 14:10)

Your son might not have a problem walking like this man Paul healed, but he might not be living up to his potential. As his mother, you have to help him rise to the identity you know he possesses.

> And when the people saw what Paul had done, they lifted up their voices, saying in the speech of Lycaonia, The gods are come down to us in the likeness of men. (Acts 14:11)

You see, sister, when you touch your son's life in a powerful way, and you do it as a single mother, it is a miraculous act that others can attribute to something less than your influence in his life. But make no mistake about it, it was you who lifted him up and gave him the courage to walk on to greatness.

> And they called Barnabas, Jupiter; and Paul, Mercurius, because he was the chief speaker. Then the priest of Jupiter, which was before their city, brought oxen and garlands unto the gates, and would have done sacrifice with the people. Which when the apostles, Barnabas and Paul, heard of, they rent their clothes, and ran in among the people, crying out. (Acts 14:12–14)

When someone wrongfully accuses you, it is natural to immediately want to correct them. Help your son be like Paul, so he understands that it is alright to help people not get things twisted.

> And saying, Sirs, why do ye these things? We also are men of like passions with you, and preach unto you that ye should turn from these vanities unto the living God, which made heaven, and earth, and the sea, and all things that are therein. (Acts 14:15)

You see, Paul and Barnabas recognized what the people were doing and who they thought them to be. But Paul and Barnabas quickly made sure these mistaken people understood their correct identity.

Sister, you know who your son is. You are with him more than anyone. Now, I know our children can sometimes attempt to live one way when we are around and live another way when we are not around. This is why you must make sure he understands that he must live out who he is in every place and in front of any group of people. The more your son is identified with positive consistent behavior and action, the more his reputation is validated. Also, it is less likely that he can be confused with anyone else or anyone else's trouble. This is what I call having an identity you can believe in.

$\mathcal{M}$ama's Story:

THE STORY OF HAVING AN IDENTITY CRISIS

Lesson: Be proud of who you are.

When I was younger, I remember being afraid of the bigger boys in our complex; they were terrors. They'd go around bullying people and accusing others of the things they had done, so these hoodlums would not get into trouble for their own actions. One bad boy in the crew, teased me, called me a momma's boy, and said he'd get me one day for the heck of it. I now know, being called a momma's boy was a great compliment coming from a thug; but back then, I was uneasy.

After telling my mom about the thug's threat, she said, "Dab, be proud of who you are. You don't have to be afraid. You are a strong man with tons of courage. Everyone knows you're a sweetheart who'd help anybody. That boy, whatever his name is, better not try anything with you or everyone around here will get 'em." Her pep talk sounded good and all, but I was still shaking in my boots. When and where was the big, bad dude going to get me?

Ironically, that same night, an episode from one of my favorite sitcoms came on—*Good Times*. You may or may not be familiar with *Good Times*. Just in case it doesn't ring a bell, let me highlight a few characters. There was James Evans, the strong and firm father-disciplinarian who said what he meant and meant what he said. There was Florida Evans, the very conservative, loving mother who always believed in doing things the right way. There was James Evans Jr. (aka J.J.), the tall, skinny, older brother who claimed to be the handsomest of the three siblings. There was Thelma Evans, the beautiful sister who was, at the highest level, a daddy's girl. Then there was Michael Evans, the youngest of the bunch, who was bright, ambitious, and had a firm grip on black history. The Evans family lived in the projects of Chicago and struggled to make ends meet.

Though I didn't have my dad in the home, I identified with the Evans' story because we also had it hard. I liked watching the show because, though things were rough for the Evans family, the tight bond they shared made life good.

In the episode I watched after my run-in with the bully, J.J. was being sought out by a bunch of strong-arm gangsters. According to them, J.J. owed them money. Well, they followed him back to his home in an effort to collect on the debt. J.J. ran inside and hid in his room. He was scared to death just as I was. When the gangsters arrived at the Evans' apartment, they ran into James, the father. (Remember, he was as sharp and hard as nails and afraid of nothing.) The gangsters asked for J.J. Mr. Evans called for J.J. to come out of his room. A frightened J. J. came out but then tried to run back into hiding. His dad grabbed him by the arm and told him he was in his own home—the one place he did not have to run from anyone.

At that moment, my mother popped me on the head and yelled out, "Tell 'em James! These boys ain't got to be scared of nobody!"

In the sitcom, James Sr. was convinced that J.J. owed those gangsters nothing. He took that position in spite of what they told him. He knew J.J. well enough to know there was no way he could be identified with such rotten characters. Sister, he was right.

This is what was crazy. As soon as *Good Times* ended, there was a knock on our door. The bully from our neighborhood, was standing there with a neighbor.

The bully screamed, "Dab's the one that broke your car window with the football. Not me. Didn't you do it, Dab?" He looked at me with a balled fist and a look that said, "Say, 'yes,' or I'll get ya."

My mother crossed her arms and gave me a glare that was even more frightening. Her look said, "Boy, if you don't tell the truth, you'll have to deal with me! And you don't want to deal with me!"

Just as in the Evans home in the show, there was no identity crisis in the home I grew up in. My mother knew who we were, and she made it her business to make sure everyone else knew, as well. Anytime someone spoke of us, my mother seemed to have her hand on the pulse of the situation. She was so familiar with our disposition, no matter what others said, she somehow knew whether it was true or not. (My brother was more outgoing and liked the social life, but he knew where the line was. My sister was very reserved and shy. I was somewhat between the two, but known for being a stand-up kid.) Mom knew us like the back of her hand. She even knew how far each us would wander away from her expectations.

Back to the story in my complex. After the guy's accusation and threatening look, I took a deep breathe, looked at our neighbor and said, "Sir, I did not break your window."

The neighbor looked at the bully, my momma, and then me. He said, "Dab, I know if you'd don' it, youda told me."

The bully got loud and insisted I'd done it. Folks started coming out of their apartments and before you know it we had a crowd. When people got wind of what I's been accused of, three ladies who sat on their porch every morning and every evening came up to the door. They explained that I was not guilty. They all confirmed who broke the window.

Later, my mother explained that our neighbor believed me because of my reputation. That bully wanted to ruin it because his was tarnished. The ladies had my back because they knew I was a good kid. They didn't want to see me in trouble for something I did not do.

Sister, this identity thing is big. Your son needs to know who he is and he needs to know that you know who he is. When that is established between the two of you, the crises will be kept to a minimum and his identity will not easily be mistaken.

From the day of that confrontation on, I didn't mind walking around my neighborhood. I kept my nose clean and the bad guys knew not to mess with the "momma's boy."

Athletic Tale

THE STORY OF THE REDEEM TEAM

Don't get it twisted, sister. Sometimes our identity gets shattered and we have to redeem ourselves. We might not have been the one to damage our own name, but because it *is* our name, we have to be the one to rid others of negative thinking about us. Your son needs to be prepared to redeem his name if ever necessary.

Since 1936, when men's basketball became a part of the Olympics, the USA team has usually dominated. Well, in 2004, the United States Olympic Basketball Team stunned the world. They didn't live up to expectations and only earned the bronze medal at the Athens Games. Now, third place in the world isn't bad. However, when you have first-place talent, coming in third is quite a letdown.

Our country's future in Olympic basketball was talked about by other countries. Our third-place finish left our competition feeling they could beat us. However, a group of men started believing they'd be on the next Olympic team. They were determined they would not let the gold slip away again.

The Redeem Team was the name given to the 2008 USA men's basketball team. You probably know some of the names that made up that team. Once I list them, you'll identify them as some of the top ballers that have ever played in the NBA: Carlos Boozer, Jason Kidd, Lebron James, Deron Williams, Michael Redd, Dwyane Wade, Kobe Bryant, Dwight Howard, Chris Bosh, Chris Paul, Tayshawn Prince, and Carmelo Anthony. They were coached by Mike Krzyzewski. This group of men was the best the United States had to offer.

You might wonder why the name, Redeem Team, was chosen. Simple, "redeem" expresses that something once lost has been restored. Once something has been lost, a redeeming effort is required to get it back.

Actually, the Bible communicates this need in reference to the condition of humanity. We were once in good standing with God. But, through the sinful choices of Adam and Eve, we lost our position of sinless connection to God. Now, our own choices cause us to be a people in need of redemption. The Bible tells us that there is but One who is capable of reinstating our connection to God and redeeming our relationship with Him. His name is Jesus, the Christ.

There are some similarities between what the "Redeem Team" represented and what Christ did on our behalf. This team was motivated to get back what the US considered to be rightfully theirs. Jesus hung on the cross for you and me, so we could once again be in a right relationship with God.

The "Redeem Team" was driven with a passion like that of Paul; they had a deep belief in who they were and in the skills they possessed. They were not to be identified with the 2004 team in any way other than the letters USA on their jerseys. Their identity was their own. They were determined take their skills and their work ethics to another level and recapture the gold for their country. As the USA faced Spain in the gold medal game, it would prove to be a tough closing act—Spain was determined to make it a fight.

However, the determination and passion of the "Redeem Team" was too much for Spain. The USA team was led by Dwyane Wade with 27 points and Kobe Bryant with 20 points. The rest of the supporting cast chipped in enough for the win—the "Redeem Team" brought the gold back to the USA with a winning score of 118 to 107. The rightful identity of the USA men's basketball Olympians was restored. As they stood center stage and held up the gold medal, they reminded the world of their true identity and whom they represented.

I'm still amazed to realize this band of basketball brothers dreamed for four years of redeeming what had taken place in 2004.

Sister, there are times in our lives when redeeming qualities are needed desperately. We just have to dig deep within, prepare, and work toward changing our fate.

Your son will have moments in his life when he will lose out on some things because his identity is tarnished. This could happen because he ruined his reputation; others who have come before him could mess him up; or certain things could be taken from him without cause. In any case, his identity will need to be reclaimed. When folks don't see him the way he wants to be perceived, the question becomes whether or not he will re-identify himself with a redeeming spirit that says, "I want back what was taken from me." To have that fighting gumption burning in his soul is one of the most needed elements of his character; it is one he will draw from for the rest of his life.

Help your son perfect the ability to keep coming back when he gets knocked down and to always establish his identity as someone who clearly wants to be, and surely is, a winner.

Inspirational Insight
Stephanie's Message

This chapter really opened my eyes. As I shared in an earlier chapter, it was important for us to give our son a new name. But now, I clearly realize the significance of helping Dustyn restore his identity.

You see, before he came to us, Dustyn was known as a young man who didn't have much hope. He was on track toward becoming a negative statistic. He was the boy known to never respond in school. (Well, if you had to wear the same unwashed, hole-filled clothes to school each day, would you have much to say?) Dustyn was the boy who was known to sleep through class. (Well, if you couldn't sleep at night because your window was broken and the cold air kept you up, wouldn't you be tired during the day?) He was known as a weakling. (Well, if you weren't eating properly, don't you think you'd dwindle away, as well?)

Sister, I'm here to tell you that God is good! He brings hope where there is none. Because God gave Dustyn to parents who cared, with God's help, we were able to build our son up and turn his life around. He is now known as the young man whose body is the best on the team. (Well, if you had a parent feeding you everything in sight so your physique would be ready for game time, you'd be on it, too.) Dustyn is known as the person who helps the less fortunate. (Well, if you experienced God's love so powerfully that He turned your whole life around, you'd have a big heart, too.) Our son is also known as the one who comes to class early and stays after school to make sure he gets his work done. (Well, if you knew you had a scholarship waiting, you'd work extra hard, too, if that's what it took.) Yes, sister, my boy has a new life and renewed confidence. Here are some nuggets that may, hopefully, help your son gain the same.

First, *teach him his identity should be in his faith*. My son came to know Christ over eight years ago. He understood God's plan of salvation, he prayed a prayer of repentance, and he placed his faith in the person of Jesus Christ. If there is any one thing you should want your son to be identified by, it should be his faith in his Savior. I believe that faith, if it is real, will drive decisions. It will pick your friends; it will influence the places you go; and most importantly, faith will get you home one day—to the home that is eternal in the presence of God. Make sure your son has a chance to understand salvation at a young age and an opportunity to place his faith in the Lord. When his identity is in Christ, nothing can rock his world.

Secondly, *teach him that his identity should be on his mind*. Help your son to be some kind of thinker. His tendencies should always err on the side of being responsible. What I mean is that your son should have a good sense of what he should and shouldn't get caught up in. Now, that doesn't mean he will always be responsible; but, if he is more inclined to think through things before he makes a choice, more of his outcomes will be favorable. If he makes the right choices up front, he won't have to be reactive and try to fix his life. When his identity is on his mind, he will make wiser choices that will ultimately help him succeed.

Lastly, *teach him to have hope in his identity*. As your son goes about life doing the right things, help him understand the great person he's showing the world will pay off—he'll be seen as a responsible man with great moral fiber. If your son has some very particular things he wants to do with his life (the way my husband wanted to play professional football), help your son understand people will help him reach his goals if they see he lives his life on the right track. A person with good character will be the one who gets ahead in life. People get behind winners. If your son wins with his attitude, with his education, and with his determination, he can rest assured phenomenal opportunities will come his way. When he has hope in his identity, he will setup a winning future because he believes he deserves one.

This book is scheduled to release around the time our son will graduate from high school. Where did the years go? Why can't I slow up the clock? Though parenting isn't easy, I'm melancholy that our time with him living daily under our roof is about to end. However, I take comfort in knowing he is not just my child, but he is a child of the King. With an identity like that, I'm much more confident as I prepare to release him.

Sister, we are all reading this book because we want the best for our sons. Yes, there is the chance that our children won't turn out the way we hope; but there is also a chance they'll turn out even better. When we give it all we've got as mothers, God will do the rest.

Remember our identity is in the Lord, as well. He knows what He's doing with you and with your son. Don't get it twisted! God is there and He cares. **He'll help you raise him, sister!!!**

recruiting

Teach

him to not

do it alone.

(Taken from Acts 16)

 Motivational Point

My wife's wise grandfather, the late, Rev. Perry, of whom I spoke in a previous chapter, would often say, "More hands make for light work." He meant the load of work becomes much easier when shared by many. This was Rev. Perry's definition of what we call delegation. It's the "I do some, you do some, we do some" mentality. If we all do a part, the job can more easily get done.

I don't mind working; but I do appreciate help to lighten the load. When my son helps me do the yard, the job gets done sooner. When I help my girls wash the dishes, the chore is finished more quickly. When my wife helps me prepare a document, the task isn't as daunting. We are all familiar with the premise, "It takes a village to raise a child."

TIME OUT!

No matter your opinion of that world view, the fact remains that no one can raise a child without aid from others. Whether in the form of teachers, friends, ministers, or childcare workers, we all need help teaching our children how to be successful adults. As we struggle with the day-to-day trials of life, we need to remember to reach out to our "village."

Sometimes, a job is impossible without the help of others. There are times when you must be willing to look for people whose assistance can help you move forward in life. If you know you have stretched yourself to your limit (and believe me, sister, we all get to that point), don't be hindered by your own limitations. When you realize you need help, find someone who can supply what you lack. No one ever gets anywhere in this life by themselves. If success is to come, in most cases, help is required. Attempting to walk through life alone is extremely difficult and unnecessary.

Asking for support from others is not a sign of weakness; it is a sign of wisdom.

Support comes in many different forms. It could be the help of a neighborhood friend who takes care of your son after school. It might be the older man in your church who offers to spend time mentoring your son. It may be the teacher who sees talent in your son and encourages him to get involved in extracurricular activities. Sister, you have to be willing to look for and recognize those people who can come beside you and give you a hand in raising your son. Seek out people you consider to be on the same wave length with you and your son. If the church has a youth group, get him involved, so the youth pastor can help him. If the school has a club or sport he'd be right for, sign him up so the sponsor or coach can help him. If a friend has a career you son is interested in, ask if he'd be willing to speak with your son and help him make a wise career choice.

Keep an eye out for talents or skills others recognize in your son. When other people comment on the abilities they see in him, please, take it seriously. Their insights could clarify some life direction for your son that you may have missed.

The insight of others was a key component to my own success and my introduction into football. Someone saw me playing outside one day and pulled me into the world of football. I have been tied to the game ever since. However, your son could get recruited into almost any area. It need not be sports; it may be a field that neither you nor your son has considered. Before Obama became President of the United States, more than likely, someone saw something in him that suggested politics as a viable road for him to take.

Raising your son alone and getting him to where he needs to be in life can sometimes require more time and ability than you have. He is growing daily; sooner than you can imagine, he'll be on his own. Right now, it's important for him to have powerful influencers in his life—people who can aid him in acquiring his dreams. It is not necessary for you to take it all upon yourself when help is all around. What may take you days, weeks, or years to get through to your son, another person may be able to teach him in hours. Why should you struggle to reach him by yourself when help is only a phone call or visit away?

There is something unique about each of us—something that distinguishes us in some form or fashion. What that quality within your son might be is the million dollar question. Think about it for a moment. What exceptional characteristics does your son possess that could be impacted by the right person to become a stepping stone into his future? What traits does he possess that might be improved and perfected to enable him to affect a lot of people positively?

Throughout your son's lifetime, certain situations will change as a result of meeting particular people; and some people will come into his life to help him change. As your son grows toward adulthood, make sure you remain watchful for the beneficial associations that come your son's way. Don't be afraid to expose him to opportunities that could be life-changing. Whether you find someone to aid your son along his path or they find him, it's always good to look deeply into the reasons each particular person has crossed his path. Far too often, the people God sends are not recognized as the priceless assistance they were meant to be in our lives. Well, I am here to tell you that God-ordained meetings happen every day. Opportunity comes in different forms and from various places—sometimes unexpected ones. You just have to keep a really good lookout for them in order to help your son navigate his path to success.

As your son's journey progresses through the years, the last thing you want him to think is that he did it by himself. Sure, he'll gain recognition for where he goes in life. However, teachers, mentors, friends, relatives, coaches, pastors, and many others deserve acknowledgment, too. No one can journey successfully through life alone. Teach him to know and honor the value others bring to his life.

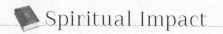

Spiritual Impact

THE STORY OF PAUL ASKING TIMOTHY TO JOIN HIM

(Acts 16:1–5)

Sister, let's keep it real; we have and will always have race related issues in this world. That's not the core of the problem. The true problem is our inability to relate productively to racial matters. The problem happens when we allow racial issues to place restrictions or limitations on our ability to connect with those who are not like us.

> Then came he to Derbe and Lystra: and, behold, a certain disciple was there, named Timotheus, the son of a certain woman, which was Jewess, and believed; but his father was a Greek. (Acts 16:1)

Now, hold on, sister; this is about to get interesting. You see, Timotheus' (aka Timothy) parents had different backgrounds. His mom was Jewish and his father was a Gentile.

> Which was well reported of by the brethren that were at Lystra and Iconium. (Acts 16:2)

You see, anytime there is an issue in a relationship, it rarely takes long for word to spread like wildfire. We know people get fired up to give and hear gossip.

> Him would Paul have to go forth with him; and took and circumcised him because of the Jews which were

in those quarters: for they knew all that his father was a Greek. (Acts16:3)

Paul knew Timothy's parents had two different back grounds; but he also knew his purpose was to win people to Jesus. Circumcision was an ancient, God-ordained custom within the Jewish culture. Anyone not circumcised was considered unclean and an outcast. Knowing the Jews would not welcome an uncircumcised, Jewish Timothy, Paul removed the barrier by circumcising him. Paul taught strongly that, in Christ, there is no longer Greek or Jew, male or female, but all are one in Him. So, we must not see Paul's circumcision of Timothy as a compromise of his convictions. Rather, Paul realized the real issue was not Timothy's physical state, but that others might come to a saving knowledge of Christ.

> And as they went through the cities they delivered them the decrees for to keep, that were ordained of the apostles and elders which were at Jerusalem. (Acts 16:4)

After taking care of what could have stood in the way of effective ministry, Paul and Timothy went about the business of teaching and preaching the truth of the gospel. Paul would not allow the customs of Jerusalem to prevent him from bringing Timotheus with him to get the job done.

And so were the churches established in the faith, and increased in number daily. (Acts16:5)

Paul's belief in Timothy was proven in the way he took Timothy under his wing and joined their lives together. As you get the chance to read about Paul and Timothy throughout the New Testament, you will discover just how deep Paul and Timothy's relationship ran. Their relationship as mentor and mentee was extraordinary. If you take a journey over to First Timothy and Second Timothy, these accounts will further clarify why Paul invested so much in Timothy.

My own son is going through the recruiting process as a potential college football player. I will confess; it has been one of the most taxing experiences I have had in a long time. The process is long and sometimes stressful. My wife and I have tried to allow him as much freedom to lead this effort as possible; but there are times when we have to step in and give some guidance. Everybody is looking for the next great athlete. It starts with the eyeball test: a player must have the right height and weight; the most important skill is foot speed. If all of these things check out, there could be a scholarship waiting on the other side; thus, making the recruiting process worthwhile.

There's nothing wrong with the right group of people taking interest in what they see in your son. Who knows what opportunity could be waiting. He just needs to keep making himself into the kind of person who warrants interest. Make sure his character is strong so he'll stand out and people will want to work with him. Teach him to be eager, have a good attitude, and be moldable.

Sister, you don't know when someone will come along and want to help your son. Timothy had no idea Paul would come. However, if your son knows up front that others can help him reach his goals, he'll be ready. If your son is ready to be recruited for greatness, he is one step closer to actually becoming great.

Mama's Story:

THE STORY OF HOW I WAS CONSIDERED A 5-STAR BY MY MOTHER

Lesson: When a mom believes, a son achieves.

If you read the title of this section, you may be wondering, "What is a 5-Star?" It's a rating grade given out by sports recruiting services. There are only five stars available. In the world of college recruiting, there are not many 5-Star athletes. To acquire this rating, an athlete's skill set must be through the roof. I'm talking at least a 94% rating. Five-Stars are considered the cream of the crop; their skill set is far above others. Every youngster who wants to go far in sports strives for this tag, but very few actually attain it. I mean, in other words (thanks Rev. Perry), 5-Star players are the highest stars.

You see, when an athlete is rated a 5-Star, everyone rolls out the red carpet and makes the greatest pitch about their school in hopes of landing him. Five-Star players have their pick of any school in the country. If a university is fortunate enough to sign a 5-Star player, it's a major deal to everyone connected to that university.

I have wanted my son to be treated in such a way. No, he is not a 5-Star football player; but he is a 5-Star son. My mother thought the same of me. She believed I was a 5-Star. She thought I deserved to be treated as though I were that rare and gifted because I was her son. There was nothing about me that wasn't 5-Star in her eyes. She would never allow me to feel inferior about my upbringing. Not even for one moment, would she allow me to think I did not have the skill set to accomplish my dreams.

When I was younger, I wanted to play recreational football. There was a team everyone in town wanted to be on. If you made that team you were a "baller." The coach was known for taking only the best talent in the city. If he didn't invite you to try out, you had a slim chance of ever making the team. Well, I told my mother about my aspirations. She said she'd take me out to the park to tryout.

Being a woman of her word, a few days later we were on our way to the park. I remembered getting sad. She asked what was wrong. I said, "Mom, the coach is known to only pick players he recruits. I don't have a chance. I don't want to try." She would not turn around. When we parked the car, I didn't want to get out. She said, "Boy, come on, here. You wanted to do this. You can do this, and this man is going to give you a chance." As we walked toward the coach, I saw boys laughing at me—either because I hadn't been invited by the coach or because I was being dragged by my momma. My mother never wavered. She tapped the coach on the shoulder and said: Sir, I heard you have the top, Pee Wee team in this area. I also heard you lost the regional champion-ship game last year. If you don't want that to happen again, my boy is a difference-maker. He is as big, fast, and as strong as anyone on this team. The coach looked at me and nodded; I passed his eyeball test. The coach said, "How come I haven't heard of him?" My mom put her hands on her hips and said: Because I'm a single mom, holding down two jobs. He's only played around the way. But he's too good to keep hidden. That's why I'm here. I need you to help make him even better. Now, you gonna give him a fair chance or what?

Coach asked me if I was ready to run some drills. I was still nervous; I felt like I didn't belong. My mom leaned in and said, "Boy, I believe in you. I've told him what you can do. Don't get out there and tip toe. Believe in yourself. You belong."

As I think back to my eleven-year-old self, I still remember feeling energized by her words. My mom believed in me so much that she made me and the coach believe. I'd never run a drill in my life; but from my top-notch performance, the coach never knew. I made his elite team. All the way home, I thanked my mom. She wouldn't take the credit. She told me, once I put my mind to it and showed my skills, I deserved to be on the team. However, I could not have made it without her.

It was this kind of confidence building from my mom that went on all the time. I have to confess, hearing her fight for me really made me feel special. Because she believed in me, I knew I had value.

If there is anyone in this world who can gave your son a sense of worth, it is you, his mother.

TIME OUT!

Sister, while your son is young, take every chance you get to communicate how special he is. The more often he hears your affirmations, the more likely it is that he'll believe you and carry confidence in himself into his adult life.

A 5-Star recruit knows he is going to be given a lot of love from those recruiting him. They will give him confidence by giving him approval and acceptance. That's what I'm talking about; love is the most powerful thing on earth. Love will overcome more than the challenges in your son's life and more than you can imagine. So, above all, love your son through your words of affirmation. Make sure you are speaking positive reinforcement into his life every single day. Make sure you let him know that he is your 5-Star. Make sure he fully grasps the fact that your love for him will overcome anything. Like my mom did for me, stand up for him when folks who can help him won't give him a chance. Feeling love from you will help him soar and be a 5-Star person.

You know what, sister? As much as I love the game of football, I will still take a 5-Star son over a 5-Star football player any day of the week and twice on Sunday. Don't you agree?

 ## Athletic Tale

THE STORY OF HOW MICHAEL PHELPS RELIED ON HIS TEAMMATES

Now, I want to make something clear right from the start. Humans are not supposed to be able to move through water the way Michael Phelps does. The last I checked, we do not have fins attached to our backs or feet. We are a dry land species. Well, someone forgot to tell Michael Phelps. Sister, I am not certain that you know who this amazing swimmer is; but, trust me, if there is anyone who could rightly be called "aqua man," Phelps is that man. Michael Phelps can move in water the way most of us move on land.

This two-time Olympian and multiple, gold medal winner is a phenomenal athlete. The Beijing Olympics was home of one of the greatest performances ever to take place—Michael Phelps fairly dominated the water as he captured eight gold medals. His performance at the Beijing Olympics was nothing less than stellar and stands to this day as one of the greatest performances of all time. Michael won five events single-handedly, but it required a very impressive group of talented swimmers to assist him in the relay efforts. The 4x100 meter freestyle relay, the 4x200 meter freestyle relay, and the butterfly relay were, in fact, a team effort.

As great a swimmer as Michael is, even he could not swim all the legs of the relay races alone. Since he could only swim one of the four legs, he was completely dependent on the other three swimmers. Surrounded by athletes with very impressive skills of their own, Michael knew how to depend on his teammates' strengths and talents to help him win the gold. Michael is the most decorated Olympian in history; he has amassed twenty-two medals, including eighteen gold. No one else in the history of the Olympics has ever accomplished this feat.

Sister, teamwork is such an important part of your son's development as a young man. Your son needs to always stay alert for moments when facing challenges alone is not the answer. The help of others can be an amazing gift.

What I love about the Olympics is that the crowning moment of the athletes' success does not arrive at the moment of victory. No, my sister. The true crowning moment of victory comes when the athlete wears the medal of achievement and stands proudly upon the podium while his or her nation's anthem plays. At this moment, the whole world witnesses a success story that was long in the making. This is the dreamed-of moment that drives the Olympic hopeful in his or her preparations.

No one can do it alone. That's right! I mean no one. Think of the race to raise your son as a relay race. This is not a single-person performance. Raising your son is a team effort between you, him, and all the other people who want to reach out and help so he can get to his winning moments in life. Recruit a team who will make your son's dreams a reality. Yes, the help of others will enable your son to move through life with ease, just like a fish (or a Phelps) easily moves through water.

Can you imagine what Michael Phelps must have felt standing there on the podium with his teammates? He must have felt grateful for the help he had in accomplishing something super special. I can only imagine what you and your son will feel when he accomplishes the things in this life that you desire for him.

Inspirational Insight
Stephanie's Message

Girl, Derrick can tell you better than anyone about recruiting. If anyone understands the importance of needing help and the inability to accomplish things alone, it's him. Derrick came from difficult circumstances; if it had not been for the help of others, he might never have found his way out. His mother helped him. His extended family helped him. His community helped him. Though they all had little to give, they all gave this boy from the projects all they had. The team effort got him out of the ghetto.

Strangely enough, my family is currently experiencing its own recruiting process. As I type this, my son is a high school football player. Colleges are interested in him, and we pray the Lord sees fit to allow him to earn a college scholarship. Regardless of what the schools think, as his mom, I know he's a heck of a player and an even better person. He would be an asset to any college program. I've been trying to instill in him the belief that his family is here, his coaches are here, his teammates are here, and his teachers are here to help. He doesn't have to reach his lofty goal alone.

Here are a few things to keep in mind that may help your son.

First, *teach him to reach up for help*. You know what I mean when I say, "teach your son to reach up"? There is no greater Helper than our Father who is in heaven. God never intended for us to do anything by ourselves. Even from the beginning, God set a precedent for working together. Adam was not created to be alone—God made him a "help meet" to walk along side of him (Gen. 2:18). God paired the disciples together as He sent them out two-by-two (Luke 10:1). There is no way He ever wants to leave us alone in life. Please teach your son to reach up to God.

Next, *teach him to reach out for help.* Reaching out requires allowing oneself to be vulnerable. However, this is not to suggest total dependence on others. Help your son understand there is no shame in asking for help or needing assistance from others. He can remain true to his own story and still lean on others for help. The worst place he can ever end up is in a place of pride where he thinks he needs no one. Girl, everything I have done has required help. Humility will enable your son to recognize his need, and wisdom will enable him to reach out to those who can fulfill that need. Please teach your son to not be afraid to reach out for help.

Finally, *teach him to reach to you for help.* I would like to share with you my "mother's creed." I love sharing it with my kids: I am here when you need me. I am here when you don't. If only you knew how much I got your back. My love for you is real. Each day you mean more. My commitment is unwavering and don't you ever question it when I tell you it's sincere.

Help your son see that reaching to you is an opportunity for you to show your great love for him. Don't let his first inclination be to reach to others (maybe even the wrong people) for help. Develop a relationship with him that causes reaching out to you first to be his immediate response to life's challenges.

Since we are on this journey together, I need to be transparent. This recruiting ordeal with my son is so stressful! Friday, we had game two out of ten games in which to impress the college scouts. One boy, who played the same position as my son, got four big plays. My son got none. I was bummed for him. But then, when I looked above for help, the Lord reminded me my son had made the biggest impact plays in the first game. My friends at the game reminded me we still have eight more games to impress the college scouts. When I looked to my Dad, who also comes to my son's games, he said, "At least he didn't have any busted plays, and he did not get hurt." Gosh, that blessed me.

My point for telling my story is this: even as a mom, you can't do it alone. Surround yourself with a team who supports you. A team can make you stronger; and when you are strong, you can help your son get stronger.

Dustyn and I talked about his last game. We agreed that, next week, he's getting me a touchdown. Now, of course, I don't know if this will happen. But, I do know that the team I have around me to help raise my son helped me be able to lift him up when he needed it. You, too, can keep connected to your team of encouragers and be strengthened to lift your son up when life gets him down. When we pump up our boys, we make a life touchdown. **Seek help in raising him, sister!!!**

a new system

Teach him

to grow.

(Taken from Acts 17)

 Motivational Point

Online banking offers a more efficient way of managing your money. Digital devices provide a more creative way to manage your life. A social media site account is a great way to communicate with the world. All these forms of digitally interacting with the world were a bit tough for me to learn, and I am still not completely comfortable with them. But once I got the basic hang of these new systems, I entered a new world. No more going to a bank for every financial transaction. No more being anchored to my desk to gain computerized assistance in managing my life.

No longer do emails to family and friends go unsent for lack of time. I am better because I adapted to a new system of operation and found a better way.

Well, sister, we are reaching the final chapters in our journey together. This is the time when the rubber meets the road. This is the time for you to consider everything you have heard to this point and decide if you are going to buy in, or not. (Of course, I believe you bought in a long time ago.) If you are to continue your effort of raising your son to be all he can be (and I know you will), the thoughts in this book offer you just a little something more to aid you in the days ahead. To some of you, these thoughts may represent a new system of operation; however, it just may be that some insights you've gained will serve as valuable tools in growing your son into the man you want him to become.

I have presented you with concepts and principles that I believe are life-proven guidelines and can serve as a support system for you if you are willing to embrace their messages. I believe the truths you've encountered here will free you up—untie your hands, and unshackle your feet—so you can build a bridge from your son's present into his future. Your son doesn't have to take a chance on walking across untried and uncertain passages; he can walk safely across the trials of life on steps you built for him.

Sister, now the ball is in your court. Are you willing to stay motivated, embrace the journey, take on the challenges, and overcome the obstacles to enable your son to embrace a winning future? I bet I know the answer to that question because I know how much you love him and desire nothing but the best for him. Boy! It's not easy, is it?

In a lot of ways, raising your son to be all he can be is like going on a long road trip across the country. As you travel, you will encounter ever-changing weather. In some places, you will encounter the problems caused by rain; but just as cars are built with windshield wipers, God will clear your vision when things in life get stormy. In other places along your journey, the weather may get stiflingly hot; but just as cars have air conditioning, God will send the cooling breeze of His Spirit when things in life heat up. You may run into some cold weather as you travel along the road. Well, girl, you can just reach down and turn up the heat in your car just like you can depend on the Lord to send the warmth of His love when icy winds blow through your life.

My hope is that what you've gained through your journey through this book will give you a better idea of how to plan your route as you travel the road to your son's future. Some of the ideas you've encountered may take some getting used to; but that's okay. Like anything, the more you practice this way of raising your son, the more it will become a normal and natural way of responding to life.

Throughout my career in football, I have often seen the ever-changing nature of the various coaching staffs. Over and over again, I have watched as one staff was fired and a new staff was hired—an old system went out and a new system was ushered in. It is always a major adjustment for the players; they must resign the old system and embrace the new system. But once the transition is made, look out!

Sister, if what you have read so far in this book has moved you, encouraged you, or even got you reenergized for the race, I say you have transitioned into a new system. It's time to take hold of all you've learned and own it. Embrace a new hope, a new way, and a new effort. Now, let me caution you sister; this new system of raising your son won't always sit well with others; but it's not about everybody, it's about the one somebody who has your heart— that young man you so desperately want to raise well.

We are not talking about my son, nor are we talking about the many other sons of the world; we are talking about *your* son. It is *your* son for whom this book is written—it's all about him. Sister, now it's time for you to go and make the living out of this new system all about him.

Each day, I get up and purposefully make that day about my children. They are gifts that God has given my wife and me, and we only have a short window of time to raise them right. They won't be children very long. Our job is to make successful adults of them—namely, to love God, others, and themselves.

I know it's a challenge; especially when you consider that each of us was born with a sin nature. But God has provided a way (a system, if you will) for us to die to that sin nature and be born anew into the kingdom of God. That "way" is Jesus, and that "system" is the salvation provided by His death and resurrection.

TIME OUT!

"For God so loved the world, that he gave his only begotten Son, that whosoever believeth in him should not perish, but have everlasting life" (John 3:16).

Above and beyond everything we teach our children, we must make sure they know this new system, this gift that God the Father has provided through Jesus the Son. If we are faithful to lead our children to receive this gift, sister, we will assure they will know the most essential and significant kind of success—a life lived with the meaning and purpose it was designed to have. I know you want that for your son.

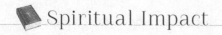 Spiritual Impact

THE STORY OF PAUL GIVING THE PEOPLE OF ATHENS SOMETHING NEW

(Acts 17:1–31)

Sister, you want to talk about a new system? Paul dropped a system like no other on the people of Athens.

> Now when they had passed through Amphipolis and Apollonia, they came to Thessalonica, where was a synagogue of the Jews: And Paul, as his manner was, went in unto them, and three sabbath days reasoned with them out of the scriptures, Opening and alleging, that Christ must needs have suffered, and risen again from the dead; and that this Jesus, whom I preach unto you, is Christ. And some of them believed, and consorted with Paul and Silas; and of the devout Greeks a great multitude, and of the chief women not a few. (Acts 17:1–4)

I don't think there are many other places in Scripture where the passion of Paul shines through so clearly. In this passage, he truly communicates to us his heart for Christ. It is this same committed faith we all hope to instill in our sons.

> But the Jews which believed not, moved with envy, took unto them certain lewd fellows of the baser sort, and gathered a company, and set all the city on an uproar, and assaulted the house of Jason, and sought to bring them out to the people. And when they found

them not, they drew Jason and certain brethren unto the rulers of the city, crying, These that have turned the world upside down are come hither also; whom Jason hath received: and these all do contrary to the decrees of Caesar, saying that there is another king, one Jesus. (Acts 17:5–7)

Paul was so passionate about what he believed that he never let up once he got started. His convictions were so strong that he was completely consumed with his mission. Sister, that's the kind of passion you need in raising your son; and it's the kind of passion for life you want to instill in him.

And they troubled the people and the rulers of the city, when they heard these things. And when they had taken security of Jason, and of the other, they let them go. And the brethren immediately sent away Paul and Silas by night unto Berea: who coming thither went into the synagogue of the Jews. These were more noble than those in Thessalonica, in that they received the word with all readiness of mind, and searched the scriptures daily, whether those things were so. Therefore many of them believed; also of honourable women which were Greeks, and of men, not a few. But when the Jews of Thessalonica had knowledge that the word of God was preached of Paul at Berea, they came thither also, and stirred up the people. (Acts 17:8–13)

Paul made it clear that there is another King above Caesar who is the Giver of eternal life. Just as many were unable to accept Paul's message as he followed the mission for his life, not everyone will buy in to the new system you are engaging to raise your son. But just as it was with Paul's mission, it's not about those who don't buy in, but about those who do.

> And then immediately the brethren sent away Paul to go as it were to the sea: but Silas and Timotheus abode there still. And they that conducted Paul brought him unto Athens: and receiving a commandment unto Silas and Timotheus for to come to him with all speed, they departed. Now while Paul waited for them at Athens, his spirit was stirred in him, when he saw the city wholly given to idolatry. Therefore disputed he in the synagogue with the Jews, and with the devout persons, and in the market daily with them that met with him. (Acts 17:14–17)

In Athens, Paul was surrounded by people who were mired in an old, destructive system. They seemed determined to hold to their mistaken beliefs. It will be much the same as you begin operating in a new mindset—a new system—for raising your son. Many people just won't get it. You will have left the old ways of thinking behind; but others will refuse to see the truth and will cling to the old way—determined you are following a wrong course.

> Then certain philosophers of the Epicureans, and of the Stoicks, encountered him. And some said, What will this babbler say? other some, He seemeth to be

a setter forth of strange gods: because he preached unto them Jesus, and the resurrection. And they took him, and brought him unto Areopagus, saying, May we know what this new doctrine, whereof thou speakest, is? For thou bringest certain strange things to our ears: we would know therefore what these things mean. (For all the Athenians and strangers which were there spent their time in nothing else, but either to tell, or to hear some new thing.) (Acts 17:18–21)

Sister, I promise you, just as Paul encountered such skepticism, you are going to draw a crowd of cynics and a great number of people will question why you are operating in a new way. You just be ready to tell them why you are embarking upon a new way.

Then Paul stood in the midst of Mars' hill, and said, Ye men of Athens, I perceive that in all things ye are too superstitious. For as I passed by, and beheld your devotions, I found an altar with this inscription, TO THE UNKNOWN GOD. Whom therefore ye ignorantly worship, him declare I unto you. God that made the world and all things therein, seeing that he is Lord of heaven and earth, dwelleth not in temples made with hands; Neither is worshipped with men's hands, as though he needed any thing, seeing he giveth to all life, and breath, and all things; And hath made of one blood all nations of men for to dwell on all the face of the earth, and hath determined the times before appointed, and the bounds of their habitation; That they should seek the Lord, if haply they might feel after him, and find him, though he be not far from every one of us: For in him we live, and move, and have our being; as certain also of your own poets have said, For we are also his offspring. (Acts 17:22–28)

For Paul, the new way was far above the old. Just so, it doesn't take much to be convinced that the old system of raising your son does not compare with the new system. Sister, don't allow you or your son to be trapped in old, destructive patterns. Always look deeply into your son's actions and attitudes. Don't let him get caught in the old system of works. Teach him it is not necessarily those who work harder who succeed; most of the time, it is the ones who work smarter who find the way to excel.

Forasmuch then as we are the offspring of God, we ought not to think that the Godhead is like unto gold, or silver, or stone, graven by art and man's device. And the times of this ignorance God winked at; but now commandeth all men every where to repent: Because he hath appointed a day, in the which he will judge the world in righteousness by that man whom he hath ordained; whereof he hath given assurance unto all men, in that he hath raised him from the dead. (Acts 17:29–31)

You see, sister? This is it—the reason God is the only One who deserves to be worshiped. You can teach your son all the techniques of this new system; but if he doesn't know the only true God, his life will never have the meaning or impact God wants for him. Above all, teach your son to worship God with his life.

God's system for new life works; and Paul's passion to convey its principles to the people of Athens was abundant, as it should be with this new system of raising your son. It will work; and your passion to head purposefully toward success for your son will soon infect his life. Not only will it make him excel, but it will also make him significant—not only to you, but to the One to whom it matters most. I think you know Who that is.

$\mathcal{M}$ama's Story:

THE STORY OF HOW SHE TAUGHT ME TO CLEAN

Lesson: Be open to new ways so more productivity can happen.

Cleaning. My mom called it "putting her skirt on." When she said those words, it was time to look out! No one could clean a house like my mom. Straightening houses and hospitals was actually the way she made her living. Some would consider cleaning to be beneath them. My mom took a great deal of pride in making things clean, neat, and orderly.

Dr. King said:

If a man is called to be a street sweeper, he should sweep streets even as Michelangelo painted, or Beethoven composed music, or Shakespeare wrote poetry. He should sweep streets so well that all the hosts of heaven and earth will pause to say, here lived a great street sweeper who did his job well.

My mother lived out those words—she did her job well.

Looking back, I now realize her system was like none other. She always thought ahead. She was what I call a "forward thinker." Her work was done in her head before it was done on site. This was her first tactic for getting her job done. My mother didn't just clean she CLEANED. She considered every detail from the ceiling to the floor. She dusted places most would not think to clean. From baseboards to crown moldings, it all had to be spotless. Every item had a place and everything had to be organized.

Mom's secret to success was her strategy. Her system was amazing. She didn't clean one room at a time. She would go back and forth from room to room until she was done. No step was wasted and very few were ever repeated.

Mom discovered a way to be effective and efficient without breaching the expectations of her employer. She firmly believed that keeping her employer satisfied was paramount. She was all about saving time and energy whenever she could; so as long as the results of her system met the approval of her employers, she had met her goal of doing her job well.

One Saturday, I had to help her clean our place. I wanted to go out and play with my friends. I was dragging. I thought my sister should clean. However, Mom said I had to help; and boy, did she mean I had to help! She had cleaned her room and bathroom while I was still straightening my closet. Mom stopped me and said, "Look, Dab. I understand you're mad; but get over it. Sometimes in life you have to do things you don't want to do so you can do things you do want to do. The faster you get your chores done, the quicker you can go play. That is, if I still let you play . . . giving me attitude about doing chores. Boy!!!" I whined, "But mom cleaning is hard. It's taking me all day to just do this part." She took over and said, "Okay. Let me teach you something. First, have a good attitude. When you're happy, you can get the job done faster. Second, think ahead. Take the sheets off of your bed and your brother's bed, and let's take them to the washer. Then you can come back and start the dishwasher. While those two things are in progress you can get other areas done. Multi-task, son. Always look for the better way of doing something."

Her words and system stuck with me. I thought it would take all day to clean the house; but we were done in three hours. Her work ethic and mindset rubbed off on me.

Sister, you know much more than your son. He may be really smart; but the life lessons you've experienced can help him find better ways of doing things. You have systems that work for you. Make sure he knows them. Seeing my mom work so smart to accomplish tasks taught me to value doing the same.

But don't let any system become a trap. You've got to be open to tweaking your systems from time to time. Your son needs to learn early to not get stuck in his ways, and to always look for opportunities of growth.

I'm so thankful my mom helped me learn a new way of cleaning and thinking. All you do for your son will be appreciated, too.

Athletic Tale

THE STORY OF COACH PAT SUMMITT AND HER STARE

The legendary University of Tennessee's Head Women's Basketball Coach, Pat Summitt, was born on June 14, 1952, in Clarksville, Tennessee. Please take a seat, sister, and listen to these accomplishments. Her head-coaching record is 1,098 wins and 208 losses—that's a .841 winning percentage. She led her team to eight NCAA Division 1 women's basketball championships (1987, 1989, 1991, 1996, 1997, 1998, 2007, and 2008), and sixteen SEC Championships (1980, 1985, 1990, 1993, 1994, 1995, 1998, 1999, 2000, 2001, 2002, 2003, 2004, 2007, 2010, and 2011). She received eight SEC Coach of The Year awards (1993, 1995, 1998, 2001, 2003, 2004, 2007, and 2008), seven NCAA Coach of The Year awards (1983, 1987, 1989, 1994, 1995, 1998, and 2004), as well as winning the Naismith Coach of the 20th Century Award and the 2012 Presidential Medal of Freedom. She was also inducted into the Basketball Hall of Fame in 2000. Her system of success starts with her, reaches forward to her players, and grows them from the floor up.

Sister, take a little page from Coach Summitt as you grow your son into the man you want him to be. She's famous for the stare she gives her players when they don't meet her expectations. If you are anything like my mom, you have a look that would freeze anyone in their tracks. More importantly, that look can grab and keep the attention of others, especially your son. No words are required. All it takes is that look. That attention-arresting stare was a part of Coach Summitt's system.

Of course, Coach Summitt had a ton of Xs and Os (also known as plays), a great team, and fantastic assistant coaches. However, it was that stare that cut right through to the core of every player who ever played for her.

Pat Summitt could coach her socks off! No one could achieve a record like hers without being one heck of a coach. I know it sounds pretty amazing, but her stare is the culmination of everything she teaches her team in the many hours of preparation before any game is ever played. The stare is a reinforcement of an existing standard. When that standard is missed, the stare shows up. The objective of the stare is not only to grow the ladies on her team into the players she wants them to be, but also grow them into the women she wants them to become. Basketball doesn't last—one day each athlete will play their last game. But the lessons from basketball will last as long as a player lives. Pat Summitt taught a ton of lessons and branded each one into her players through the heat of her stare. If her players were to list the lessons they learned from Coach Summitt, they would, no doubt, attribute the power of recall to her commanding stare.

As Coach Summitt taught her teams, teach your son to operate within your system. Make sure he understands what your system is about. Once he understands it, he will strive to operate within it. If you have no system, your son will learn to come and go as he chooses and have no real pattern for a successful life. Take a lesson from Coach Summitt. Her players were expected to play within her system. If you wonder whether establishing a system for your son will work, just look again at the achievements of the teams Pat coached. Let her success and the subsequent success of her players act as a reminder that sticking to your guns works.

Sister, we are approaching the end of our time together. I want you to know that I am cheering for your success and your son's success. Even if nothing I have shared thus far helps, I know prayer will.

TIME OUT!

A system isn't just a plan of action, it can also be a way of thinking and believing.

Pat Summitt's way was powerful. She worked hard. She surrounded herself with the best. And her stare was empowered with the influence gained through determined leadership of her teams. Stay on your son! Don't let him get away with conveniently "forgetting" the lessons you've taught. Train your eyes on him, and make him face the truth in your eyes. All the days of his life, he will never forget your stare of love.

Inspirational Insight

Stephanie's Message

Wow, wow, wow! I am moved by what I just read. I gotta get a stare of my own. I've got to teach my son my system. I am pumped. I hope you are, too.

I get the chance to read each of these chapters before I write my little part and try my best to contribute to this book. As I read and as I write, I pray for you. I hope this book speaks to your heart, so you can help your son achieve greatness.

Here are three points I hope you can use to lead your son to success.

First, *teach him to stay with the new system*. I know learning a new way of responding to life can be difficult; sometimes you can feel overwhelmed. But remember, sticking things out is usually worth all the headaches. Two very good things happen when we try the new way: (1) we know the new way is better, so we're stronger from the knowledge; (2) as we implement the new plan, it will prove itself, and we will grow stronger because we are better equipped. When you refuse to try a new way, you will never know the power new knowledge can bring.

Secondly, *teach him to seek the new system*. When your son is open-minded, he can expand. When he expands, he can achieve more. Tell him about folks like Steve Jobs, the creator of the iPad. Your son may be the one who finds the next great thing to improve future lives. Make sure your son looks for more in his life: more answers, more solutions, and more of God's love. Help him understand that worldly systems may change with the times, but God's system won't change. When your son understands more about God and His Word, he can operate within a system that is dependable and unchanging.

Lastly, *teach him to tell others about his new system*. That's right! I mean exactly what I just said. When everybody else is looking for answers, your son will have the knowledge. Tell him to share it. Teach him early in life how to be a leader. Help him clarify his thoughts and implement his plans. Be his helper, and share his dreams. With the God-given ability we have as mothers, we can enable the next generation to be better than the last.

Honestly, this chapter challenged me. I am involved in five writing projects as I'm doing this one. The pressure is on me to complete it all. This chapter has inspired me to look for better ways to tweak my own system. Am I doing too much? Do I need more help? Do

I need to just keep my head down and churn out the work? Yes, yes, and yes. So I'll reevaluate and tweak my personal system, so I'll be better prepared to help my son develop his own. I encourage you to do the same.

We need to be at our best so we can help our young men be even better. Grab on to the new plan to which you've been introduced. Find a new and better way of doing things. And invent a new system, and perfect that stare. (Gosh! I love Pat Summitt's stare.)

The bottom line is this: just as you picked up this book to help you find a new way to parent your son, keep on seeking new methods to help you in all areas of life. **A better you can more successfully raise him, sister!!!**

going for it

Teach him

to not

turn back.

(Taken from Acts 27)

✦ Motivational Point

Well, sister, this is my last message of encouragement and insight for you and your son. It may be the end of this journey; but it may mark the beginning of a brand new life for you and that young man.

Sometimes, you have to weigh life on the scales of opportunity. You must decide what you are going to do with those unexpected or subtle events that arrive without warning. They can either leave you shaking your head or wiping your eyes. You may not have control over those events, but you can develop the ability to manage those events. As you walk from today into your future, you will encounter things that can catch you by surprise and shake you from your seat. At times, the strength of your resolve will be greatly tested. The fact that you will be tested by unexpected events is not a popular or even a welcome topic. But it is one that must be covered because the journey before you can be long and challenging.

Now, you may be wondering why I waited until the end of this book to mention trials and challenges. Well, I'll tell you why. Simply put, because I believe you have bought in to the concepts and approaches written in this book and you are ready to press on and never give up. I believe your resolve is more powerful than any challenge you may face.

Now is the time to fix your eyes on your goals and set your affections on your son. It's time to move forward. Don't get overly concerned with what may go wrong. You see, sister, wrongs can be made right. Rather, look at how far you have already come. I would be willing to bet, your mindset has changed and your perspective has been altered by the time we've spent together gleaning from God's Word.

It's time now to go for it! It's time to dig deep, grab hold of your son, and help him become the person that you and others will respect and greatly appreciate. You have come so far; you have gleaned many worthwhile messages, and you have been given powerful tools to use in the task set before you—to raise a godly, successful, young man. It is my fervent hope that you don't turn back or revert to the lesser things of the past. Instead, I pray you move forward with all the energy and stamina within you.

It would be foolish to compare football with far greater or more serious events in life; but for the sake of making sure you are with me, please bear with yet one more sports analogy.

Coaches in football are often faced with the necessity of choosing to keep the offense on the field and go for it on fourth down or punt.

TIME OUT!

The offensive players are responsible for moving the ball down the field. They push forward against all opposition to reach their goal.

Coaches weigh the situation and consider every possible way to keep the offense on the field. Even though it may be more advantageous to punt, coaches often realize it is still more important to keep the offense on the field. Thus, many times they go for it. They dig in, set their sights on the goal, and resolve to maximize offensive plays.

You see, sister, going for it is sometimes a better option than giving the ball back to the other team. It really takes courage and a great belief in your own abilities to do this.

What I am trying to tell you is that this is no time to punt; sister you have to go for it.

There are certainly things that will show up along your journey that will be difficult, things that can and will change your life with less than a moment's notice. What will you do when this happens? How will you respond in these situations? Let me tell you the one answer that has served me well. To make it through the unexpected and difficult episodes of life, you must have resolve. This word denotes coming to a decision or having one's mind made up to find a way to press on, no matter how difficult the situation has become.

Let's face it, this life is filled with things and situations and circumstances that reshape or redefine our perspective. This does not mean that we have to stop or give up on where we are headed. It just might mean we have to pull over, catch our breath, and resolve to go on.

The journey to raise your son may seem long and can certainly be difficult. Sister, I want you to really get this. You may already have hit a bump in the road; you may have hit many. That's okay. From now on, in tough times, take a deep breath, put one foot in front of the other, and keep going. It's this kind of resolve that will allow you to rebuild your life when circumstances tear you down. It's this kind of resolve that says, "I will not be moved by this event! Instead, I will trust in the Lord."

Believe it, sister! There is no clean sailing across the oceans of life. However, there is Someone who has conquered the raging sea. I think you know to whom I am referring. The great Jesus! He wants to be a strong presence in your life. And the Helper, who is the Holy Spirit, is your companion as you take this giant leap of faith with God.

Sister, God wants to help you and give you a real future and a hope (see Jer. 29:11). Look to Him for wisdom and direction as you raise your son. Let God be your "go to" person. He is truly the Difference Maker today, tomorrow, and forever.

In my mind, I can see you shouting. You go, girl! No. Better yet, you go for it! And, come what may, teach your son to go for it, too.

 Spiritual Impact

THE STORY OF PAUL BEING CAUGHT IN A STORM

(Acts 27:9–44)

Along the journey toward this new life, you will meet obstacles that you will be forced to manage, or they will manage you. Difficulties and barriers will challenge your resolve. Just as Paul pressed on through hardships throughout his life, so you must also press on through it all. Facing every obstacle and resolving to forge your way through is one of the most valuable lessons you can teach your son as life unfolds.

> Now when much time was spent, and when sailing was now dangerous, because the fast was now already past, Paul admonished them, and said unto them, Sirs, I perceive that this voyage will be with hurt and much damage, not only of the lading and ship, but also of our lives. Nevertheless the centurion believed the master and the owner of the ship, more than those things which were spoken by Paul. (Acts 27:9–11)

Paul faced danger head on; he did not shy away when difficulties threatened. Sister, I want to make sure you know that there are dangers and risks involved in many areas of life. But when trouble shows its ugly head, do not be fearful and do not be weary. More rewards than dangers await us when we tackle the trouble and confront the trial. We must deal with whatever comes if we seek to arrive at a better place.

> And because the haven was not commodious to winter in, the more part advised to depart thence also, if by any means they might attain to Phenice, and there to winter; which is an haven of Crete, and lieth toward the south west and north west. And when the south wind blew softly, supposing that they had obtained their purpose, loosing thence, they sailed close by Crete. But not long after there arose against it a tempestuous wind, called Euroclydon. And when the ship was

caught, and could not bear up into the wind, we let her drive. (Acts 27:12–15)

Paul and the crew of the ship found themselves caught in a storm. They did whatever they could to make it through, but the storm raged around them regardless of their efforts. Sometimes, when we step out, we come face to face with trouble. We may find that no matter what we do, we cannot avoid it. At those times, we must do our best to simply hold on and resolve to make it through.

And running under a certain island which is called Clauda, we had much work to come by the boat: which when they had taken up, they used helps, undergirding the ship; and, fearing lest they should fall into the quicksands, strake sail, and so were driven. And we being exceedingly tossed with a tempest, the next day they lightened the ship; and the third day we cast out with our own hands the tackling of the ship. And when neither sun nor stars in many days appeared, and no small tempest lay on us, all hope that we should be saved was then taken away. (Acts 27:16–20)

Just as Paul and his shipmate-captors found themselves tossed mercilessly by a fierce storm, so we may find life raging and threatening to overwhelm us. Concern and worry can grip us and cause us to be fearful. Yet we know the One who calms the storms. Keep praying, keep your calm, and keep going.

But after long abstinence Paul stood forth in the midst of them, and said, Sirs, ye should have hearkened unto me, and not have loosed from Crete, and to have gained this harm and loss. And now I exhort you to be of good cheer: for there shall be no loss of any man's life among you, but of the ship. For there stood by me this night the angel of God, whose I am, and whom I serve, saying, Fear not, Paul; thou must be brought before Caesar: and, lo, God hath given thee all them that sail with thee. (Acts 27:21–24)

Paul understood that faith is the opposite of fear. By placing his trust in God, he was able to stand strong in the face of danger. Sister, take a lesson from Paul. Your greatest comfort should be the presence of your God and Lord. He will speak to your heart and assure you that you can weather any storm because He is your Shelter and your Deliverer.

Wherefore, sirs, be of good cheer: for I believe God, that it shall be even as it was told me. Howbeit we must be cast upon a certain island. But when the fourteenth night was come, as we were driven up and down in Adria, about midnight the shipmen deemed that they drew near to some country; and sounded, and found it twenty fathoms: and when they had gone a little further, they sounded again, and found it fifteen fathoms. Then fearing lest we should have fallen upon rocks, they cast four anchors out of the stern, and wished for the day. (Acts 27:25–29)

Take a lesson from Paul. When trouble brews, be of good cheer. Keep moving even when you fear the worst and it appears you can go no further. Keep reminding yourself that you know the One who can fix anything.

> And as the shipmen were about to flee out of the ship, when they had let down the boat into the sea, under colour as though they would have cast anchors out of the foreship, Paul said to the centurion and to the soldiers, Except these abide in the ship, ye cannot be saved. Then the soldiers cut off the ropes of the boat, and let her fall off. And while the day was coming on, Paul besought them all to take meat, saying, This day is the fourteenth day that ye have tarried and continued fasting, having taken nothing. Wherefore I pray you to take some meat: for this is for your health: for there shall not an hair fall from the head of any of you. (Acts 27:30–34)

Paul urged the men on the ship with him to get a grip. When they were ready to desert the ship, he assured them that they would be fine if they would follow the Lord's directions. Sister, there may be times when it seems your life is in the same kind of stormy turmoil that frightened Paul's captors. The only way to make it is to keep the faith through the winds of adversity and the waves of doubt. Keep the faith in your Lord; He will always bring you through the storms. Keep the faith in your son as he learns to weather life's storms. He needs to know you believe in him and you don't plan to abandon ship.

> And when he had thus spoken, he took bread, and gave thanks to God in presence of them all: and when he had broken it, he began to eat. Then were they all of good cheer, and they also took some meat. And we were in all in the ship two hundred threescore and sixteen souls. And when they had eaten enough, they lightened the ship, and cast out the wheat into the sea. And when it was day, they knew not the land: but they discovered a certain creek with a shore, into the which they were minded, if it were possible, to thrust in the ship. And when they had taken up the anchors, they committed themselves unto the sea, and loosed the rudder bands, and hoised up the mainsail to the wind, and made toward shore. (Acts 27:35–40)

When left to our own devices, we can fall far too easily into despair. It's important for both you and your son that you remain connected to the Source of all comfort—our Lord. Thankfully, you and your son are a team. You can encourage and comfort one another as you ride through the storms life sends your way. Take advantage of all opportunities to encourage him, and allow him to encourage you.

> And falling into a place where two seas met, they ran the ship aground; and the forepart stuck fast, and remained unmoveable, but the hinder part was broken with the violence of the waves. And the soldiers'

counsel was to kill the prisoners, lest any of them should swim out, and escape. But the centurion, willing to save Paul, kept them from their purpose; and commanded that they which could swim should cast themselves first into the sea, and get to land: And the rest, some on boards, and some on broken pieces of the ship. And so it came to pass, that they escaped all safe to land. (Acts 27:41–44)

Even when land was in sight, Paul's captors remained in the grip of fear. Their only hope was to keep their eyes on the shore and focus their energy on getting there in one piece. In this story, we get a bird's eye view of what matters most in arriving at that future land of promise for you and your son. Sister, no matter how difficult the situations you face, resolve to believe that you and your son are going to make it. You go for it, and make sure he follows your lead.

If God be for you (and we know He is based on Rom. 8:31–39), and your son is with you (and we know you'll never leave him behind), well, what are you waiting for? The time is right and the time is now. Get on board to begin your adventure! I can only imagine your success as you raise your son to heights beyond the stars.

Mama's Story:

THE STORY OF MY MOTHER'S RESOLVE

Lesson: Keep yourself together so you can push on.

This particular story is an emotional one for me. As I write these words, I struggle to keep it together. I hope by now you have had a chance to appreciate my mom. She is and will always be so special. Don't get me wrong. The three women in my house are incredibly special, as well. But this story is not about them; it's about my mother.

My mom gave all she had in raising her children, and I am forever grateful for her commitment to me and my two siblings. Her story is amazing! Wondering how she managed all she faced still staggers my mind. The only logical explanation for her dynamic approach to life on our behalf is love. My mother loved us; that love was the driving force behind her power as a woman and her passion for her children. Let me share why I feel this way.

You see, sister, all my life my mother has been devoted to her responsibilities as a parent and as a mother. She was born poor in her pocket but rich in her character. Hers is a story of what it is like to work for thirty-two years on the same job, doing exactly the same work day after day. She never complained. In fact, she loved her job because it enabled her to take care of us.

Mom worked every day, rising early in the morning to start each day with worship before she prepared breakfast for her children. She always made sure we had something to eat before she left for work. The morning meals she prepared stuck to my ribs; my favorite was homemade biscuits, crispy bacon, and scrambled eggs. But there were many mornings when we had to make do with cornflakes and water. (Milk was sometimes not within mom's meager budget.) But with or without money, Mom always took care of business the best she could; she was always on point.

TIME OUT!

"On point" means to be ready to perform to the greatest level, or to be ready to get down to business.

I remember Mom's maid's uniform. She wore it with pride. I loved watching her walk out the door every morning. She had such pep in her step. My mom and her best buddy would meet up at the bus stop, always excited to start a new day.

Life was certainly not easy for my mother. But there were only a few occasions when I saw the difficulty she faced.

Mom was a disciplinarian and had the task of keeping two boys at bay. If only you knew of the whippings I received. Those are outlawed in today's world. Maybe that's the problem with today's world, because those spankings got me straight.

I remember rushing in to Mom's room one day to tell her I'd gotten an A on the math test she had helped me study for. I was stopped dead in my tracks when I saw tears streaming down her face. As her son, my heart broke. Who or what had hurt my mom so badly, and how could I fix it? When she saw me, she immediately wiped her eyes and tried hiding her raw emotions. I went over to her and said, "Mama, please tell me what's wrong?"

Etched in my brain, I remember her saying, "I wish your dad was here. I've got to do this on my own baby. But we're gonna be alright. Yes, we are." Interestingly, she was talking to me, but she was also talking to herself. I now think she was also talking to God.

I didn't inquire on that day or any day before or after about her relationship with my father. I've never known or sought to know why they were not together. But I do know that, once Mom came to grips with the truth, though her heart was broken, she kept herself together. Like a lioness leads her cubs through the jungle, my mom led us through our wilderness. On her own, she protected us, feed us, clothed us, nursed us, and taught us. What drove her was her devout love for three people who each lived inside her for nine months and with her for the rest of her life. My mother is, without a doubt, a very special woman.

Sister, I know you feel my mother's story. I know you can identify with her. In many ways, her story is your story. Though specifics may be different, you walk the same road she traveled before you. As you go on from this book, let her story inspire you to never turn back. Let the lessons she taught with her life help you teach your son to always reach ahead to grasp his dream and fulfill God's purpose for his life.

Athletic Tale

TONY DUNGY SURVIVES THE STORM

I have had the great honor of meeting the great, former football coach, Tony Dungy. When he was the coach of the Tampa Bay Buccaneers and his team played the Atlanta Falcons, I was provided the opportunity to speak at their chapel the morning before their game. There is no one more gracious on the face of the earth than Tony Dungy. When you meet him, you get the impression that he really wants to know you and sincerely cares for you.

There's a statement I use often that sums up people like Tony Dungy: "Never let your success or fame rise higher than your faith." Living out this statement is what makes Tony Dungy unique to his profession and strikingly similar to his Lord and Savior Jesus Christ. There are so few people like him walking the face of the earth.

You see, sister, something life-changing happened to Tony Dungy. Something so devastating that I almost feel inadequate to relay the story. James Dungy, Tony Dungy's oldest son, died three days before Christmas in 2005.

Tony had to face the unthinkable challenge of going on without his son. Yet, he had to lead his team, the Indianapolis Colts, no matter the personal anguish he faced. Tony Dungy knew the meaning of a life storm of incredible magnitude; but he somehow found the internal resolve required to press on through unimaginable heartache.

Tony's resolve to persevere and his strength through the ordeal helped us all get through those sorrowful days. He showed incredible strength when he spoke his dear son's eulogy. Tony and his family operated with nearly superhuman compassion by choosing to donate James' organs to those in need of life-giving transplants. He not only continued coaching his team, with unbelievable determination and stamina, he led them to a Super Bowl win. Through the most devastating loss, Tony Dungy operated with resolve, perseverance, strength, compassion, determination, and stamina. Only by the grace of God could a father's heart find the vigor to face such overwhelming loss with such fortitude and courage.

Tony has often said that he has not totally recovered. However, because of his faith and the fact that his son knew God, Tony faces life each day with the same qualities he displayed during the harrowing hours following his son's death. With all Tony knows about heaven and the kingdom of God, even if he could bring his son back, he wouldn't. Tony, thank you for being an example we all can strive to emulate.

Sister, I hope the message of Tony Dungy's life reaches you wherever you are today. May the same resolve, which is a result of faith, strengthen you as you face the challenges of life in raising your own son.

It's good to be a great coach and an awesome parent; but above all, be absolutely certain that you and yours are saved.

Sister, if Tony can press on, we all can. May God help you and move you to a place where you want to be.

Inspirational Story
Stephanie's Message

Well, girl, let me try to put this last chapter into perspective. It will be difficult because I am overwhelmed with emotion. At the same time, I am filled with great joy. Reading Derrick's mother's story and Tony Dungy's story impacted me with a powerful message that touches at the core of my being. I hope what Derrick has written over these chapters has inspired you to fight on.

To hopefully end on a high note, I thought I would leave you with something different than usual. Previously, I have closed with three points that impacted me; but I thought it would be a fitting end to pull points for this last chapter from the African American National Anthem, *Lift Every Voice and Sing* (words written by James Weldon Johnson). This anthem means much to me personally because it is the imprint name for many of my young adult books. May the words in this anthem move you, too, and always help you and your son go for it.

> First, *teach him to lift up his head and rejoice when he needs strength to carry on.*
>
> Lift every voice and sing, till earth and heav'n ring,
> Ring with the harmonies of liberty;
> Let our rejoicing rise, high as the list'ning skies,

Let it resound loud as the rolling sea.

Sing a song full of the faith

that the dark past has taught us,

Sing a song full of the hope

that the present has brought us;

Facing the rising sun of our new day begun,

Let us march on till victory is won.

Secondly, *teach him to remember his forefathers when he
needs inspiration to carry on.*

Stony the road we trod, bitter the chastening rod

felt in the days when hope unborn had died

yet with a steady beat, have not our weary feet

come to the place for which our fathers sighed

we have come over a way that with tears has been
watered

we have come treading a path through the blood of
the slaughtered

out of the gloomy past till now we stand at last

where the white gleam of our bright star is cast.

Lastly, *teach him to seek his heavenly Father when he
needs help to carry on.*

God of our weary years, God of our silent tears

thou who has brought us thus far on the way

thou who has by thy might led us into the light

keep us forever on the path we pray

lest our feet stray from the places oh god where we
    met thee

lest our heart drunk with the wine of the world we
    forget thee

shadowed beneath thy hand

may we forever stand

true to our God, true to our native land.

If you teach your son this anthem, and make sure he knows its message, he can go on from anything. Know you are worthy of being his mother. Know you can do the job of helping him reach his dreams. Know God is with you. Oh, how far have our forefathers brought us! And, oh, how far your son can go! **Raise him, sister!!!**

Conclusion

I dare not trouble you much more, though I hope you have enjoyed the time we've shared. It has been a pleasure to take you on this journey and to have the honor of touching the lives of you and your son.

Sister, you may have to go the distance on your own. That's okay. Just remember God has given you the stamina to complete the race. My prayer and hope is that somewhere in these twelve chapters you have found the inspiration, the courage, and the practical advice that will empower you and give you an even greater passion for raising your son. May every point from every chapter make a difference in your efforts to see your son become the successful man you dream he will be.

I said I would be brief, and I plan to do just that. May God bless you and keep you in His perfect peace. **Go raise him, sister!!!**

Also available from THE SISTERS IN FAITH

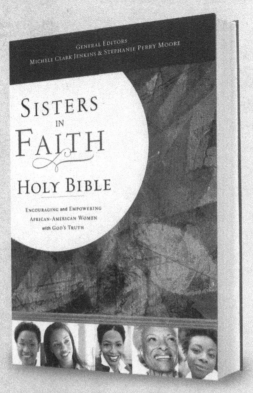

The Sisters in Faith Holy Bible MAKES THE BIBLE ACCESSIBLE TO THE AFRICAN-AMERICAN WOMAN.

Executive editors Michele Clark Jenkins and Stephanie Perry Moore seek to highlight where the Bible speaks to the five major areas of life: God, Family, Others, Self, and Career.

Additional contributors include recording artist Joann Rosario Condrey, novelists Kim Cash Tate, Vanessa Davis Griggs, and other scholars and artists committed to encouraging and empowering African-American women with God's truth.

For more, visit www.thesistersinfaith.com.

AVAILABLE WHEREVER BOOKS AND BIBLES ARE SOLD.

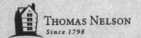

THOMAS NELSON
Since 1798

BE FILLED WITH

God's Abundant Peace

9781400322534

God's Wisdom® for *Sisters in Faith* brings encouragement amidst the struggles and demands of life. Featuring devotional content from the *Sisters in Faith Devotional Bible* as well as Scripture readings, this book addresses important topics all women face, such as abiding in God's love, being anxious in nothing, praying for one another, and developing strength for the journey.

AVAILABLE APRIL 2013